First Gentleman's COOKBOOK

Compilation and Commentary
by
William D. "Bill" Orr
First Gentleman
State of Nebraska

Project Coordinator/Editor
Pamela Holloway-Eiche

— 1989 —

Printed in the United States of America
by
Jacob North Printing Company, Inc.
Lincoln, Nebraska 68510

FIRST EDITION

Book Design, Cover Photography and Typography
by
Ayres and Associates, Inc.
Lincoln, Nebraska 68506

This book is dedicated to men who have yet to discover how satisfying it can be to start from scratch and serve a good dish or two...

Bill Orr

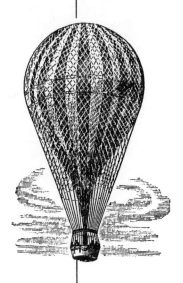

Additional copies of the First Gentleman's Cookbook may be obtained by using the tear-out order forms inside the back cover or by writing to:

First Gentleman's Cookbook
Governor's Mansion
Lincoln, Nebraska 68508

Please enclose your return address with a check payable to First Gentleman's Cookbook in the amount of $12.50 plus $2.50 per book for shipping and handling. Nebraska residents add $ .76 sales tax per book.

The proceeds from the sale of the First Gentleman's Cookbook will be used to establish the Governor's Mansion Restoration Foundation, a permanent, non-profit endowment for future restoration and redecoration of the State of Nebraska's "official residence" at 1425 H Street, Lincoln, Nebraska.

ACKNOWLEDGEMENTS

In long past idle moments I recall wondering what "history" would remember Pam Eiche for, if anything. The thought never occurred that it would be for helping provide a way to replace the gold flocked wallpaper (and other decorative oldies) in the Governor's Mansion via the proceeds from the sale of this book.

So be it. I'm not picky. And it's certainly better than some alternatives that might be considered. While "history" may select a different achievement to memorialize these other people, nonetheless, they should also be remembered and thanked for their contributions to this effort.

First and foremost, Bill Orr, who was as nice to work with as anyone could ask. But then he always has been. His idea for this cookbook was superb... his enthusiasm was contagious...and his scotch was a lifesaver at the end of some long days.

A large measure of gratitude to all the people who contributed recipes and candid photographs as requested. After all, what would Bill have had to compile—or I have had to edit—without them? A disclaimer, however, to those hopefully thousands of you who read this book and actually cook any of the contents. Not all of the recipes have been "kitchen tested". If you have a complaint, please direct it to the contributor, not the coordinators.

A "rose" to Governor Orr, too, whose guidance occasionally got Bill and me rightly refocused when there was so much to look at we couldn't see anything.

To Bill Smith and the other Mansion Restoration Foundation Fellows who had the courage to put their money where my mouth was—bless you. May all your loans be repaid in full. (Order forms may be found inside the back cover!)

Ann Andrejack, Bill's secretary, proved to be an invaluable pivot for the exchange of information, a willing research assistant and provider of encouraging words. No wonder Bill raves about her capabilities.

Natalie Cross Peetz, Deb Schoor and Marilyn Hasselbalch in the Governor's Office always answered questions cheerfully—as if they didn't have anything else to do!

Sincere thanks to Attorneys Keith Prettyman and Tom Fischer whose professional guidance helped launch the Governor's Mansion Restoration Foundation and put the cookbook project on a legally correct course.

Then, what are friends for? In this case — proofreading. My absolute appreciation to Roberta (Bert) Haefner, and Ruthann Young for their attention to this somewhat thankless, definitely tedious and always time-consuming task. The syntax and spelling in The First Gentleman's Cookbook are better for their help.

For 25 years, I've had the support of thoroughly professional and personable co-workers at Ayres and Associates, as well as Jacob North Printing. Not one of them let me down this time either. But then, they never have. Thanks, troops — you do nothing but get better.

And finally, the biggest thank you to my little family of Mom, Fred and Hardy, who got short-changed in terms of my attention for several months. Your understanding and patience will not go unrewarded — I will now return to the kitchen on a more regular basis. I just bought this great new cookbook, you see....

Pam Eiche, Editor

A blessing for the beginning-

Give us, Lord, a bit o' sun,
a bit o' work and bit o' fun.

Give us in all the struggle and sputter,
our daily bread and a bit o' butter.

Give us health our keep to make
and a bit to spare for others' sake.

Give us, too, a bit of song
and a tale and a book to help us along.

Give us, Lord, a chance to be
our goodly best, brave, wise, and free.

Our goodly best for ourselves and others
till all people live as sisters and brothers.

An Old English Prayer

TABLE OF CONTENTS

THOUGHTS ON BEING THE FIRST GENTLEMAN AND AUTHORING A COOKBOOK OF THE SAME NAME—

It all started before I became First Gentleman...

More than 30 years ago, I married a great cook and baker. The result? I became "addicted" to good home cooking.

About 10 years ago, Kay decided to get serious about politics. She became the Governor's Chief of Staff and later was appointed State Treasurer. She then ran for the office of State Treasurer and won.

I had a decision to make—did I learn to cook or did I eat restaurant and store-bought food? As Bob Dole recently put it when his wife, Elizabeth was appointed Secretary of Transportation in the Bush Administration, "I suppose it's back to TV dinners for me; but I'll probably still vote for her confirmation".

They say life begins when the youngest child leaves home and the dog dies. In our case, that was about three years ago. I was really looking forward to life "beginning". Shortly thereafter, Kay decided to get two more dogs and run for Governor. (I don't think that's what "they" had in mind...).

During Kay's campaign for Governor, several people across Greater Nebraska commented, "I suppose when Kay gets elected, you'll do a cookbook." I said, "Sure!" That one word, "Sure!", started the whole thing. The cookbook took on a life of its own. It turned from a colorful possibility into a campaign promise. And I, like Kay, believe keeping campaign promises is a good idea.

National attention was focused on the Nebraska Gubernatorial campaign because two women were running against one another for the first time. Media coverage from both coasts and foreign countries was not uncommon. The net result was (and is) that Nebraska has had a great deal of attention directed toward itself and its people.

(continued)

Immediately following the election, Kay was interviewed on network television. I was standing off to the side holding her purse behind my back and was photographed in that position by Associated Press. The photo appeared in virtually every daily newspaper in the United States and many newspapers abroad. In the weeks that followed, I heard from a number of my friends with whom I hadn't had contact in years. They sent the clipping, along with their version of the appropriate caption — many of which could not be reprinted here.

What is it like to be First Gentleman? Men have a difficult time trying to figure it out. That is understandable, since most men (including me) think of themselves as head of the household. There have been some interesting remarks, but none more amusing than one from a young lady cashier at the local bank. Since I seldom stop at that branch, this cashier had never seen me before and I had never seen her. Upon looking at my name, she said, "Do you mind if I ask you a question?". I said, "Go ahead". Her first question was, "Are you the wife of the Governor?", whereupon she blushed bright red and sputtered, "What I meant is, are you Mr. Kay Orr?".

So here I am — whatever you care to call me — hoping you enjoy half as many laughs and favorite new recipes as I have because of this cookbook. Who knows? If it's a success, maybe I'll decide to do The First Gentleman's Second Cookbook....

Bill Orr

FIRST GENTLEMAN'S FARE

Many, if not most, of the great chefs in the world are men. Aside from the few great chefs, however, most men are afraid to venture into the kitchen. Some of us have discovered that cooking can be fun. There are some recipes which are favorites of mine...and that I feel very comfortable preparing. These are the ones that follow.

APPLE CAKE

Bill Orr

2 eggs
2 cups flour
2 cups sugar
1 cup oil
1 tsp. vanilla
2 tsp. cinnamon
½ tsp. cloves
¼ tsp. nutmeg
4 cups sliced apples

Mix ingredients by hand. (Might as well get some exercise while you're learning to cook!).

Place in 9x13 baking pan, greased. Bake 45-50 minutes at 350°.

Frost with combination of:
4 oz. softened cream cheese
3 tbsp. melted butter
1 tsp. vanilla
1½ to 2 cups powdered sugar

Several years before I learned to cook, I learned to bake. To be specific, I baked a cake once a year on Kay's birthday. Each year I had to go back and ask which one was the teaspoon and which one was the tablespoon. (When you only do something once a year, you don't get very sharp at it...) Out of 10 cakes, at least 8 of them turned out the way they were supposed to. They were all started from scratch and this taught me a fair amount about reading recipes out of cookbooks. I never baked the same cake twice...but this is one of the ones I've done several times since...changing a little thing here or there till it's "perfect".

CELEBRATE NEBRASKA BURGERS

Bill Orr

1 lb. hamburger
1 small onion, minced
1 small potato, grated with peel
½ cup bread crumbs
¼ cup milk
1 egg
1 tsp. salt
½ tsp. medium grind black pepper

Mix and form patties. Spray grill or broiler surface with "Pam" to prevent sticking. Actually, they work best if you put a sheet of aluminum foil on grill, spray that, and then cook burgers.

❧

This is the recipe that won 3rd place at the Beef Cookoff at the State Fair in 1988. It's actually an adaptation of a very old recipe called "Depression Burgers" that was made during the 30's using the grated potato as a meat-stretcher. Pretty interesting stuff, huh? Bet you didn't think you'd get a history lesson as a bonus when you bought this book! (Incidentally, if you want to buy more copies for friends, you'll find order forms inside the back cover. Remember, it's for a good cause and tax deductible, too!)

CHEESE-EGG STRATA

Bill Orr

Layer in 9x13 pan sprayed with "Pam":

4 cups white bread cubes with crusts cut off
8-10 oz. package of grated cheddar cheese
2 cups cubed ham
½ cup melted butter

Beat together:
6 large eggs
4 cups milk
2 tsp. prepared mustard
½ tsp. salt
¼ tsp. white pepper

Pour mixture over layers. Set in refrigerator overnight. Dust top with paprika, place in 350° oven for 45-50 minutes. Serve with salsa.

You can also vary this recipe by adding other ingredients such as diced bell pepper, mushrooms, crumbled bacon, etc.—if it sounds good, it will probably taste that way (at least to you!).

CHICKEN SALAD

Bill Orr

1 cup diced cooked chicken
1 cup frozen peas, thawed
½ cup diced celery
½ cup chopped green onion
½ cup Spanish peanuts
¼ cup chopped green pepper
1 cup mayonnaise mixed with 1 tbsp. lemon juice

Mix ingredients. Refrigerate overnight. When ready to serve, stir in one can of Chow Mein noodles. Or, it's also nice served on a bed of Chow Mein noodles.

And—that's right…¼ cup Spanish peanuts DOES belong in this recipe. It's not a typographical error…it's a gastronomical dare that you'll be glad you took. Really adds to the flavor.

CHILIS CON QUESO DIP

Bill Orr

½ cup finely chopped onion
2 tbsp. margarine
29 oz. can of tomatoes, drained and chopped
16 oz. Velveeta or American processed cheese
small can diced green chilis, drained

Saute onion in margarine for 5-10 minutes. Add drained tomatoes and drained chilis and cook over low heat 15 minutes. Mash with fork. Add cubed cheese and stir until melted. Keep warm and serve with tortilla chips.

❦

I make this wonderful concoction every time I hold a meeting of the RGH Club. This is a club I founded, because as you know, there aren't very many First Gentlemen in the United States. As a matter of fact, the only other one is Arthur Kunin, husband of Madeline Kunin, Democratic Governor of Vermont. Since Kay is the first Republican woman Governor of a state, this makes me the first Republican male spouse or First Gentleman. That's why I founded RGH (Republican Governors' Husbands) Club. I hold meetings whenever I want. The agenda and mission of RGH are extremely secret. Nobody, including me, knows for sure what RGH is up to. (Other than good eating, that is...)

CORN CHOWDER

Bill Orr

3 tbsp. each finely chopped celery, carrots and onion.

Saute vegetables lightly in a little butter. Add a little water and cook till tender.

Add 1 can of creamed corn and 1 can of milk.

Throw in a dash of Worcestershire sauce and a dash of Lawry's Seasoning Salt.

Heat and serve.

I asked for the original of this recipe from the Elks Club in Fargo, North Dakota, several years ago. They very willingly gave it to me. Trouble was, it started out, "Take 4 pounds of butter...." Well, I knew right then I'd have to do a little revising of the quantities...but after a couple of trials, I got it down to manageable proportions that would fit in a pot we owned. If you're having a crowd, you can double, triple or magnum-expand this to suit the number and your available utensils.

CRABMEAT MOLD

Bill Orr

3 cans crabmeat
1 cup Miracle Whip
1 cup half and half
1 envelope Knox unflavored gelatin
1 tsp. chopped green onion or chives
2 tsp. Worcestershire sauce
¼ tsp. salt
¼ tsp. white pepper
¼ tsp. lemon juice

Heat half and half and add gelatin...stir till dissolved. Remove from heat, add rest of ingredients and pour into mold sprayed with "Pam".

Now the absolute truth about this recipe is that it is my absolute all-time favorite hors d'oeuvre. This is what Kay always made me on MY birthday, along with an icy-cold martini. Ah, what bliss! Only trouble was, we always had company, and I never got to eat enough of it. Well, a few years back, when I got home from work, there it was on the table by my favorite chair. A WHOLE crabmeat mold and a chilled martini. Kay said, "There it is—all for you—Happy Birthday!". Whereupon, just as I had my first mouthful, 50 people burst through the front door and said, "Surprise!". I didn't get much of it that time, either. That's when I decided to learn to make it myself, so I could have one whenever I wanted it.

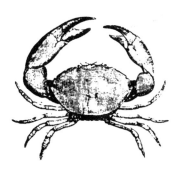

FETTUCINI VERDE

Bill Orr

6 tbsp. butter or margarine cut in chunks
1 cup chopped green onion
2 cloves garlic, minced
3-4 cups hot cooked and drained noodles
(NOT green ones)
1 cup whipping cream or half and half
1 cup Parmesan cheese
salt and pepper
ground nutmeg

Use a wok. When wok is hot, add butter. When butter has melted, add onion and garlic. Stir-fry until onion is limp. Add cooked noodles and cream. Stir to mix over high heat until cream just begins to boil. Sprinkle with cheese, then toss and mix until noodles are well-coated. Season with salt, pepper and nutmeg to taste. Pass additional cheese to sprinkle over, if desired.

❦

So what's wrong with using an Oriental utensil to make an Italian dish? It works wonderfully well. Don't get hung up on conventional methods...after you've spent some time at "home on the range", you may get an idea about a better way to cook something. Go ahead and try it...and be sure to let me know if it works!

GOVERNOR'S LOAF

Bill Orr

1½ lbs. ground beef
2 tsp. horseradish
5 tbsp. BBQ sauce or catsup
½ cup chopped onion
2 tsp. dijon mustard
1 egg

Use your hands and "squish" the ingredients as though you were making a mud pie. Put the mixture into a loaf pan and bake for 60-75 minutes at 325°.

As my good friend Bill Smith says, "The only thing better than meat loaf is a meat loaf sandwich". I couldn't agree more. I guess this is my most-shared recipe. It has appeared in the KFOR Holiday Cookbook, "Wishbone Alley" (the Nebraska Make-A-Wish cookbook), and a couple of other places, I think. Everyone so far has seemed to enjoy it...hope that includes you, too.

MOM'S POTATO SALAD

One of my favorite dishes is potato salad. Most men hesitate to make it because of a number of critical steps that may "seem" difficult; namely, cooking the potatoes and deciding the number of eggs for the amount of potatoes, as well as the quantity of salad dressing. Here is my "secret" (thanks to my mom):
Bill Orr

---

3 potatoes (prefer red)
4 hard boiled eggs (always one more egg than potatoes)
chopped onion (¼ cup to ½ cup)
mayonnaise and salad dressing (prefer equal parts)
1 tsp. yellow prepared mustard
dash of Worcestershire sauce
pinch of sugar
splash of vinegar

DON'T OVERCOOK THE POTATOES. Peel them, cut them in half, boil until a fork can penetrate without difficulty. Set off burner, pour water off—they continue to cook even though out of water.

Cut potatoes into smaller pieces, mix in hard boiled eggs and add mayonnaise/salad dressing mixture. Key point: you can always add more, but start with ¼ cup each. Add onion and balance of ingredients. Taste and add additional mayo/dressing if too dry.

It is best to allow potato salad to sit in refrigerator for an hour or two before serving.

❧

A lot of people submitted recipes from their mothers or grandmothers...and this is my addition to that category. Mom died last summer while we were beginning to put this book together and I know she'd be pleased to be included. I wouldn't have it any other way.

POT ROAST

Bill Orr

Sear pot roast on both sides in electric fry pan.

Add ¼" water.

Cook slowly, 225-250° for 3½ to 4 hours.

For last hour of cooking add potatoes and carrots.

(Hint: wash the potatoes and leave skins on, but peel the carrots...otherwise they will have a bitter taste.)

See how easy that is? And there isn't a better simple meal around anywhere. Also makes good sandwiches later.

TROOPER'S RIBS

Bill Orr

Country-style pork ribs,
carefully chosen for lean, not fat content...

Place ribs on broiler pan in oven at 450° for 30 minutes.

Take out ribs, pour off excess grease, then roll and slosh with
your favorite sauce. (I prefer Hunt's All Natural BBQ Sauce.)
Cover. Reduce heat in oven to 300° and bake another 30
minutes.

Take out, reroll, reslosh, recover and return to oven at 300°
for another hour. (Perform previously described "R&Rs"
after half an hour has elapsed.)

❧

This recipe got renamed after I made it in the Mansion for
the first time. About the time they had been cooking long
enough to start smelling REALLY good (which they do), I
noticed the state troopers assigned to the Mansion started
wandering by the kitchen door...and began hanging around
hopefully. Now, whenever I make ribs, I make enough extra
for...yep, you guessed it...the "troops". (MEN: if you want a
recipe with which to start your cooking career – this is IT!)

SWEDISH RYE BREAD

This recipe has been made for generations of Swedes in my family. It was given to me by my Grandmother Skoglund. Only trouble with it is that I don't have time to make it often enough now.

Kay A. Orr, Governor of Nebraska
Lincoln, NE

Combine:
4 cups rye flour
4 cups hot water
1 cup sorghum
⅔ cup brown sugar
1 tbsp. salt
4 tbsp. shortening

Soften:
4 tbsp. yeast in ½ cup water

Mix all of above together to make a "sponge". Put in warm place and let rise for 1 hour.

Knead in 7 cups of white flour, divide dough into four loaves and let rise until double. Bake at 350-375° about 40 minutes.

WDO: What can I say about the "First Lady" in my life? If it weren't for her, I'd never have learned to cook and where would that have left this project?

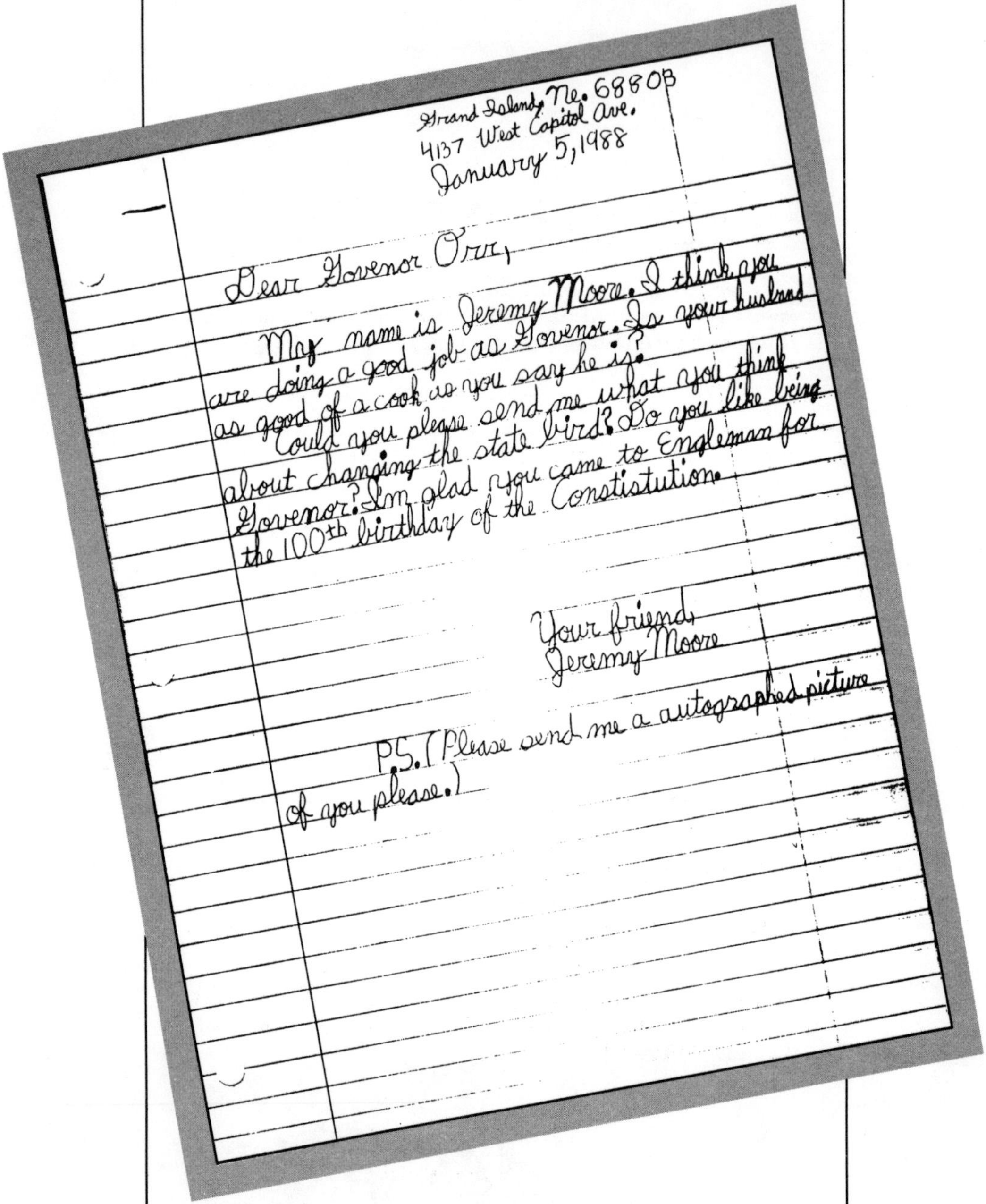

Grand Island, Ne. 68803
4137 West Capitol Ave.
January 5, 1988

Dear Govenor Orr,

My name is Jeremy Moore. I think you are doing a good job as Govenor. Is your husband as good of a cook as you say he is? Could you please send me what you think about changing the state bird? Do you like being Govenor? Im glad you came to Engleman for the 100th birthday of the Constistution.

Your friend,
Jeremy Moore

P.S. (Please send me a autographed picture of you please.)

18

GOVERNOR'S MANSION RESTORATION FOUNDATION FELLOWS

The recipes in this section are contributed by men brave enough to back the publishing of this book. Since this is a charitable cause, we can only conclude that their willingness to do so was motivated by charity and friendship. We are eternally grateful for their support and realize they provided it for two reasons: 1) the aforementioned charitable considerations and 2) the chance to get their favorite recipe published.

GRILLED
LEG OF LAMB

Every now and then a beef lover needs a change of pace.
George Abel, President
NEBCO, Lincoln, NE

Ask your butcher to debone and flatten a leg of lamb to a thickness of 1″ to 1½″. Visible fat and membrane should be removed. It will dress down to about 4 pounds. Generously brush with French dressing and marinate for 1 to 2 hours.

Place lamb on grill. During cooking, brush often with dressing. After 10 minutes, turn the meat and continue to turn until the lamb is pink. It should be ready in 20-25 minutes. Serves 10.

❦

WDO: George has been the leader of Abel Construction for years. His contributions to the University of Nebraska are legendary. As a member of Woodmen's Board of Directors, he keeps us on our toes. And—it's been said he could pave the entire state of Nebraska in one afternoon if given the order to do so.

ATTITUDE READJUSTMENT

Harold W. Andersen, Chairman/CEO
Omaha World-Herald, Omaha, NE

Start with yet another out-of-town trip by a civic-minded wife.

Stir in a husband who doesn't even like to cook steaks on a backyard grill.

Allow husband's feelings to simmer as he reflects that this is the fourth trip his civic-minded wife has taken in the past six weeks.

Stir gently—very gently.

Allow husband's feelings to cool as he discovers his wife has left a chilled martini glass for him in the fridge.

Add a dash of chilled martini—no, make that two dashes of chilled martini, on the rocks with a lemon twist.

Pop a Banquet frozen meatloaf dinner into the microwave.

Microwave for 5 minutes.

Take Banquet dinner and remnants of chilled martini into family room.

Relax and enjoy dinner, martini and the evening edition of the Omaha World-Herald.

WDO: Andy is pretty candid about his ability to cook. What he lacks there, he more than makes up for in his role as a community leader (his wife, Marian, isn't the only volunteer in the family).

EMERALD CITY SALAD

A good party salad because you do the whole thing ahead of time.

Dale M. Jensen, Executive Vice President
Information Technology Inc.
Lincoln, NE

1 large head lettuce, torn into bite-size pieces
1 cup chopped celery
4 hard-cooked eggs, sliced
1 10 oz. package frozen peas, partially cooked
½ cup chopped green pepper
1 bunch green onions, chopped
2 cups mayonnaise
8 slices bacon, crisply fried and crumbled
4 oz. cheddar or colby cheese, shredded

In a large clear glass bowl, layer all ingredients in order beginning with lettuce. Refrigerate 8 hours or overnight.

WDO: Dale has enjoyed well-earned success as one of the two leaders of Information Technology. While rarely quiet in a crowd, he has quietly given much back to his community and state in the form of service and support.

GRANDMOTHER LINCOLN'S BEST BLACK OIL CAKE

Don't let the title mislead you—this is a lovely, moist cake you will enjoy.

George A. Lincoln, Owner, Lincoln Industries
Lincoln, NE

Combine:
¾ cup salad oil
1 cup buttermilk (or milk and vinegar)
2 egg yolks
1 tsp. vanilla
Sift:
2 cups flour
2 cups sugar
1 tsp. baking powder
¼ tsp. salt
1 tbsp. soda
scant ½ cup cocoa (unsifted)
Add:
1 cup boiling water

Mix and pour into oblong pan. Bake at 325° 40-50 minutes.
Icing: Basic Buttercream Frosting

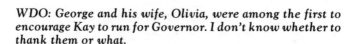

WDO: George and his wife, Olivia, were among the first to encourage Kay to run for Governor. I don't know whether to thank them or what.

STEAK JEROME

To make this recipe, you must divest yourself of past predetermined feelings about what you should NOT do to expensive beef tenderloin. Interested? Read on...
Jerry Mapes, Chairman, Mapes Industries
Lincoln, NE

2 lbs. beef tenderloin
2 sticks butter (margarine if you are in the bypass club)
2 garlic buds, diced
14 oz. can tomatoes, drained and diced
½ cup green garden onions or shallots, diced
1 cup beef broth
8 to 10 sliced fresh mushrooms
¼ cup Madiera wine
Optional: 4 to 8 oz. vodka
trace of vermouth
2 olives

Melt the half pound butter (or margarine) in a large skillet. Saute the chopped up garlic, onions and mushrooms on low heat until tender. Add chopped tomatoes and beef broth. Let mixture simmer on low heat while you prepare the tenderloin as follows:

Slice tenderloin into 1″ thick slices. Now comes the great psychological barrier that you must overcome. You must pound (yes, pound) that priceless tenderloin into ¼″ slices.

Add the Madiera to skillet and raise heat until mixure is bubbling. Drop meat into bubbling mixture and cook for about 1½ minutes per side. Pour into serving bowl and serve on warm plates.

Note: the optional vodka portions are very helpful if you have a hang-up about flattening beef tenderloin. Drink up – don't add it to the recipe!

❧

WDO: Jerry and I start Saturdays visiting with a group of men over breakfast at K's Restaurant. This group could take over Lincoln—or perhaps the world—except for one thing. No two people ever agree on anything. Jerry and I also shop at Ideal Grocery, not just for the food, but for the sage advice that is given to those who shop there.

25

HAM AND
POTATO SALAD

Described as "a meal in itself"...not to be confused with the
chapter of the same name found on page 327.
Dallen Peterson, Founder, Merry Maids
Omaha, NE

10 medium potatoes—boiled, peeled and cubed
6 hard-boiled eggs (save 2 for garnish)
2 cups diced celery
1 chopped onion
1 cup sharp cheddar cheese cubed
3 cups boiled ham cubed
1 head saussy or celery cabbage
(save nice leaves for garnish
and shred the rest)

Dressing:
¾ cup salad oil
1 cup mayonnaise

Combine dressing mixture. Toss lightly with salad ingredients. Serve on large platter with sliced eggs on top. Sprinkle with parsley. Put wedges of tomato, radishes, carrot sticks
or curls around border.

WDO: Dallen and wife Glynnis made a very big success of
Merry Maids in a relatively short time. An acute sensitivity to
people, a flair for administration and boundless energy may
have helped. I could've used some help from one of their Merry
Maids when I first started cooking, but I've gotten better about
making such a mess (now that I know I have to clean it up...).

WILD RICE CASSEROLE

This is delicious served with wild game or used as a turkey stuffing. Each Christmas we give this recipe and a pound of wild rice to friends.

William C. Smith, Chairman/CEO
FirsTier Financial, Inc.
Lincoln, NE

1 cup uncooked wild rice
3 cups chicken broth
2 cups chopped celery
1 cup chopped onion
4 oz. can sliced mushrooms
1 can cream of mushroom soup
⅓ cube margarine
1 tsp. poultry seasoning
½ to 1 tsp. salt
¼ tsp. pepper
½ tsp. sage

1. Stir rice into boiling chicken broth. Reduce heat, cover and simmer for 35-45 minutes until rice puffs open and is tender. Pour off excess liquid and fluff lightly with a fork.

2. Blend soup, melted margarine and seasonings.

3. Mix all ingredients in a covered casserole dish.

4. Bake 1 hour at 350°. Serves 6-8.

❧

WDO: Bill is known as perhaps the most outstanding banker in Nebraska. To us at Woodmen he is Christy's father. She is the cheerful cashier who brightens the day of anyone enjoying the Woodmen cafeteria at noon. Bill is also the guy who lined up the financial backing for this book. Hope he doesn't live to regret it. (Order forms available inside back cover!!!!)

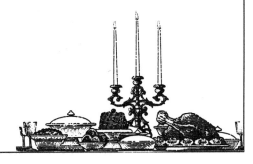

CHICKEN GORGONZOLA WITH CURRANT SAUCE

An extraordinary entree for entertaining everyone.
Gene Spence, Chairman, OPPD
Omaha, NE

---

skinned, boned and pounded chicken breasts

fold gorgonzola cheese inside each chicken breast and seal edges with mallet

dredge breasts in flour then dip into egg and milk wash

saute in butter then bake in oven at 350° for 15 minutes

saute one minced shallot in pan in which chicken was sauteed

deglaze with white wine

add to deglazed pan:
> 1 package Knorr Swiss Oxtail Soup per recipe
> red currant preserves
> black currant preserves

heat until hot and pour over chicken

WDO: Gene is one of Nebraska's leading citizens and formulator of opinion. He has been an advisor to Governor Orr and many others both in and out of state government. His viewpoint is valuable despite what you might think when you see his picture on page 318.

BAKED EGGS

My 30-and 40-year olds still come home and ask me to fix these. The recipe is a derivation from the ones served on the dining car that ran between Lincoln and Chicago.

Dale Tinstman
Eaton, Tintsman, Druliner, Inc.
Lincoln, NE

2 eggs
2 links sausage
1 slice cheddar cheese
1 piece of bread
lemon pepper
Worcestershire
paprika
Durkee's (optional)

Cook sausage in fry pan until nearly done. Tear crust from bread. Place remaining bread in bottom of oiled or greased baking dish. (4½" diameter pyrex or similar size). 2-3 drops Worcestershire on the bread. 2-3 drops sausage drippings on the bread. Break eggs in dish. Season to taste. Place 2 link sausages in whites of eggs. Bake at 425° for 18-20 minutes. Place cheddar cheese slice on top—also Durkee's if used—and bake another 3-4 minutes. Use knife to cut around edge of dish—place on plate—dash with paprika and serve.

❧

WDO: Dale is one of the pioneers of Nebraska economic development. One best way to describe him is that every time he has tried to "retire", his corporate parents have talked him out of it. Assuming his ability to cook is as good as his ability to turn businesses into successes, I recommend his recipe.

WHITEHEAD WHOPPER

*Put on your apron: look through the "fridge" and cupboards.
Create and chop up a storm.*
Bus Whitehead, CEO, Whitehead Oil Company
Lincoln, NE

Mix:
1½ lbs. ground chuck with one egg, garlic powder,
Worcestershire sauce,
57 sauce, chopped onion and bleu cheese.

Pat:
into large circle about the size of a pieplate

Spread:
on one-half the circle: chopped dill pickle, grated sharp cheddar cheese, capers, mushrooms (OR: make up your own
filling)

Fold:
over and seal edges shut

Broil:
over hot coals 7-8 minutes on each side

Serves:
3 gluttons

Aftermath:
promise wife (girlfriend) vacation if she'll clean up the
kitchen.

🌳

*WDO: Between Standard Oil, Shell Oil, Texaco and Bus White-
head, some 90% of the U.S. oil market is collectively controlled.
In Nebraska, Bus is Phillips 66. Before that, he made quite a
reputation in basketball. This reputation was made before the
basketball was "round". Although Bus was quite good at the
time (he has even been inducted into the Nebraska Sports Hall
of Fame), his reputation has improved as people who were
around then left Nebraska, died, or lost the ability to remember precisely.*

SPECIAL
SESSION
SECTION

Nebraska has 49 state senators. It is the only Unicameral legislative body in the United States. While all were asked, not all Senators contributed a recipe. However, those who did prove that some Senators can cook as well as write. (Does this mean that some can do neither?) For sure, the State Senators all enjoy a good meal—I have personally witnessed that!

CHICKEN AND NOODLES

This recipe is the one used at the Sarpy County Republican Soup Supper every year...one of Bill Orr's favorites!

Emil Beyer, 3rd District
Gretna, NE

---

12 lbs. chicken (raw weight)
3 cups chopped onions
3 cups chopped carrots
3 cups chopped celery
⅓ cup salt
1½ tsp. garlic powder or granules
2 tsp. pepper
3 1-lb. packages of noodles
(or equivalent frozen or homemade noodles)

Cook chicken. Remove from broth and cool enough to work with it. Remove skin and bones and chop into small pieces. Into broth put vegetables and seasonings. Cook until tender. Return chicken to broth. Add noodles about 20 minutes before serving. This is thick. If a soup is desired, use fewer noodles. Yield: one electric roasterful.

WDO: We got to know Emil and Barb because he is a State Senator. However, we got to know them better because he makes the best chicken and noodles ever! How can anything so good also cure you in the finest Jewish Grandmother tradition?

SOUR CREAM CHOCOLATE CAKE

Harry Chronister,
Former Senator, 18th Dictrict
Schuyler, NE

1½ cups sugar
½ cup Crisco
2 squares bitter (unsweetened) chocolate, melted
2 eggs
2 cups flour
½ cup sour milk (to sour, add 1 tbsp. vinegar to milk)
1 cup boiling water
Add to water 2 tsp. baking soda

Mix sugar and shortening. Add eggs, then chocolate and sour milk. Add flour and water with baking soda, alternating until both are used. Bake 25 minutes at 325°.

Frosting:
2 cups powdered sugar
2 tbsp. oleo
half and half (add enough to
make spreading consistency)
2 squares unsweetened chocolate, melted
1 tsp. vanilla

Add as listed and beat until smooth.

BARBEQUED WALLEYE

The Late Robert Clark
Former Senator, 47th District
Sidney, NE

1 or 2 walleye pike fillets
4 oz. barbeque sauce
¼ cup chopped onions
¼ cup chopped green peppers
1 cube butter
salt and pepper to taste

Put fish in aluminum foil, add rest of ingredients. Fold foil to seal. Put on barbeque for 20 minutes.

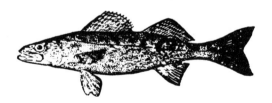

RHUBARB CHEESECAKE PIE

This recipe is used on special occasions...it is sinfully delicious.
Gerald Conway, 17th District
Wayne, NE

9" unbaked pastry shell
3 cups finely diced rhubarb
¾ cup sugar
1½ tbsp. flour

Stir rhubarb with sugar and flour mixture until coated. Put into pastry shell and bake at 425° for 15 minutes. Remove from oven and lower temperature to 350°.

8 oz. softened cream cheese
2 eggs
½ cup sugar

While pie is baking, beat the cream cheese. Add the eggs, one at a time, beat well after each. Add sugar, mix well and pour over hot rhubarb layer. Return to oven and bake at 350° for 30-35 minutes. Remove from oven and spread the following mixture on hot pie:

¾ cup sour cream
1 tsp. vanilla
2 tbsp. sugar

Cool well before serving. Refrigerate leftovers.

HOT CHICKEN SALAD SANDWICH

A different approach from the standard "cold" chicken salad. Try it!

Glenn Goodrich, 20th District
Omaha, NE

2 cups chopped chicken
1 cup grated cheddar cheese
⅓ cup chopped celery
¼ cup slivered almonds
½ cup mayonnaise
1 tbsp. minced onion
1 tbsp. lemon juice
salt to taste

Combine all ingredients. Spread on buttered buns and wrap individualy in foil. Refrigerate until ready to heat and serve. Bake in 375° oven for 15-20 minutes. Makes 6-8.

RED, WHITE
AND BLUEBERRY
PARTY SALAD

*Here's one that's perfect for the fourth of July...cool, colorful
and "company-fied" to boot.*
**Mrs. Elroy (Carol) Hefner, 19th District
Coleridge, NE**

1st layer:

>   3 oz. package raspberry jello
>   2 cups hot water

Dissolve gelatin in hot water, pour in 9x13 pan and chill till
firm.

2nd layer:

>   1 envelope unflavored gelatin
>   ½ cup cold water
>   1 cup half and half
>   1 cup sugar
>   1 tsp. vanilla
>   8 oz. package cream cheese softened
>   ½ cup chopped nuts (optional)

Soften gelatin in cold water. Heat cream and sugar together
till hot but not boiling. Place all ingredients in bowl (except
nuts if used) and blend till smooth. Add nuts and pour over
first layer. Chill till firm.

3rd layer:

>   3 oz. package raspberry jello
>   1 cup hot water
>   1 1 lb. can blueberry pie filling

Dissolve gelatin in hot water. Add pie filling and pour over
first two layers. Chill until firm.

Cut in squares to serve.

ONION DARK RYE BREAD

Make a Reuben sandwich on this bread and you've got something really special (and substantial!).
Clarence E. Jacobsen, Former Senator, 33rd District
Hastings, NE

1 envelope dry onion soup mix
1¾ cup water
3 tbsp. dark molasses
3 tbsp. vinegar
3 tbsp. lard, butter or margarine
2 tsp. caraway seed
4 cups all purpose flour
4 cups dark rye flour (preferably Rye Graham)
⅓ cup sugar
3 tbsp. cocoa
2 tsp. salt
2 packages rapid rise dry yeast
¼ cup warm water
2 eggs, beaten
melted butter or margarine

Combine onion soup mix, 1¾ cup water, molasses, vinegar, lard and caraway seed in sauce pan and heat to warm (110°). Mix flour, rye flour, sugar, cocoa and salt. Soften yeast in ¼ cup warm water. Stir warm onion liquid into 2 cups flour mixture. Stir in softened yeast and eggs.

Gradually add balance of flour mixture to make a moderately stiff dough. Turn dough on to a floured board and knead until smooth and elastic. Place in greased bowl and let rise for approximately 45 minutes. Punch dough down and form into four loaves for french pans, two loaves for 9x5 pans. Cover and let rise for 45 minutes. Bake 40 minutes at 350° in french pans or 45 minutes at 350° if in 9x5 pans.

After baking, let stand for 10 minutes and remove from pans. Brush crust with melted butter or margarine and cool on wire rack.

SALMON LOAF WITH PIQUANT SAUCE

This was one of the first dishes my wife fixed for us after we were married. It's still one of my favorites.
Lowell C. Johnson, 15th District
North Bend, NE

Loaf:
1 1-lb. can salmon, drained and flaked
2 cups soft bread crumbs
1 tbsp. chopped onion
1 tbsp. melted butter
½ tsp. salt
½ cup milk
1 slightly beaten egg

In a bowl combine salmon, crumbs, chopped onion, butter and salt. Combine milk and egg; add to salmon mixture and mix thoroughly. Shape into a loaf on greased shallow baking pan or in loaf pan. Bake at 350° for 35 to 40 minutes. Serve with Piquant Sauce or creamed green peas. Makes 3 or 4 servings.

Sauce:

Cook 2 tbsp. chopped green onion in 3 tbsp. butter till tender, but not brown. Blend in 2 tbsp. all purpose flour, ½ tsp. dry mustard, ½ tsp. salt and a dash of pepper. Add 1¼ cups milk and 1 tsp. Worcestershire sauce. Cook, stirring constantly, until sauce thickens and bubbles.

PIEROGI

This dumpling recipe originated in Poland and was brought to the United States by my parents. It continues to be a favorite in our family...which if you look at the photo on page 250, you will see is a large one!

Bernice Labedz, 5th District
Omaha, NE

Dough:
2 eggs
½ cup milk
2 cups flour
½ tsp. salt
1 tsp. melted butter

Stir and mix together dough ingredients. Knead until firm. Let dough sit for 10 minutes covered in a warm bowl. Divide dough in half and roll thin. Cut in 4″ circles with round cutter. Place 1 tbsp. of filling of your choice on each circle of dough, moisten edge of circle with water, fold over and press edges together FIRMLY. Make sure circles are well-sealed to prevent filling from escaping from the dumpling. Drop "Pierogi" into salted boiling water. Simmer gently for 5 minutes. Lift out with a slotted spoon. WARNING: Do not overcrowd pierogi when cooking.

Prune Filling:	Sauerkraut Filling:	Cottage Cheese Filling:
1 cup prunes	2 cups kraut	1 cup dry cottage cheese*
1 tsp. lemon juice	Rinse kraut and chop slightly.	dash salt
1 tsp. sugar		1 tsp. lemon juice
Soak prunes overnight; simmer until tender.		1 tbsp. sugar
		1 whole egg
		1 egg yolk

* If creamed cottage cheese is used, force through sieve to eliminate liquid. Cheese must be free of moisture.

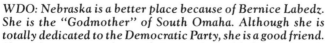

WDO: Nebraska is a better place because of Bernice Labedz. She is the "Godmother" of South Omaha. Although she is totally dedicated to the Democratic Party, she is a good friend. She is also a generous human being to a host of dedicated friends and followers.

ON THE LAMB

Howard Lamb, 43rd District
Anselmo, NE

1. Open a can of beans.
2. Spice it up with leftover steak.
3. Heat and eat.

This is the extent of my culinary abilities!

WDO: Howard has got to be kidding! We have enjoyed being "on the Lamb." Fortunately, Jo did the cooking.

THICK AND SAVORY CLAM CHOWDER

This goes together quicker than you might expect...and it goes well with a nice slice of fruit pie.

Dan Lynch, 13th District
Omaha, NE

2 cans (6½ oz. each) minced clams
2 cups finely diced potatoes
1 cup finely chopped onion
1 cup finely diced celery (or 1 tsp. celery salt)
¾ cup butter or margarine
¾ cup flour
1 qt. half and half
1½ tsp. salt
½ tsp. pepper

Drain liquid from clams and pour over vegetables. Add water to barely cover and cook until tender. Melt butter; add flour and spices and blend well. Stir in half and half and cook, stirring until smooth and thickened. Add undrained vegetables and clams and heat through.

DAD'S CHOCOLATE COOKIES

During my years growing up in North Platte, my father worked on the railroad and my mother did all the cooking with one exception. My dad did know how to make chocolate cookies. He had learned from his parents and on special occasions he would prepare his chocolate cookies for us. My two brothers and I now carry on this tradition...

James McFarland, 28th District
Lincoln, NE

1 cup sugar
½ cup butter
2 eggs
2 cups flour
6 level tbsp. cocoa
½ cup sour milk (1 tbsp. vinegar added to regular milk)
1 tbsp. vanilla
1 tsp. salt
1 tsp. soda
1 cup walnuts
1 cup cooked raisins

Mix sugar and butter well. Add eggs and stir. Add 1 cup flour, cocoa and stir. Add sour milk and stir. Add one more cup flour and stir. Add vanilla, salt, soda and stir. Add cooked raisins while hot, chopped walnuts and stir. Grease cookie sheet with butter only once. Heat oven to 350° and then turn down heat to 300° so cookies won't burn. Drop onto cookie sheet by tablespoonsful. Bake on the average of 15 minutes. Recipe makes about 3 dozen cookies.

❦

WDO: On opening day of the 1988 Legislature, Jim had the misfortune to lock himself in a restroom in the Capitol Building. He was eventually rescued. Later that day, Kay presented him with a "churchkey" tied with a large red bow. The attached note read, "so you won't ever get locked in the can again". A good bipartisan laugh was had by all, including Jim.

CINNAMON ROLLS

These cinnamon rolls are one of the many reasons I married my wife, Mary.

Jerry D. Miller, 37th District
Davenport, NE

1 cup boiling water
½ cup sugar
½ cup margarine
1 tbsp. salt
2 cups cold milk
2 eggs
2 packages yeast
9 cups flour

Pour boiling water over sugar, margarine and salt. Stir. Add 2 cups of cold milk and yeast. Stir until yeast is dissolved. Add eggs and beat with mixer. Add 4 cups of flour and beat again. Let this stand 15 minutes. Beat again and then stir in remaining flour. Turn dough out on floured surface and let it rest 10 minutes. Knead and let rise until double. Divide dough into 3 parts. Roll each into a 6 x 12" rectangle. Spread margarine on each. Cover each with a cinnamon-sugar mixture of ½ cup sugar and 1½ tsp. cinnamon. Roll up and cut each into 12 equal portions. Place in 3 pans that have been prepared with sticky mixture as follows:

Sticky for 1 pan:
½ cup butter
½ cup brown sugar
2 tbsp. cream
chopped nuts (optional)

Melt butter, add brown sugar and cream, pour into pan. Sprinkle with nuts if desired.

Let rolls rise until double. Bake at 350º for 25-20 minutes.

SCOTTY'S HARVEST TIME BARS

Get a big glass of milk and dig in!

Scott Moore, 24th District
Stromsburg, NE

---

1 cup margarine
2 cups oatmeal
1½ cups flour
1 cup brown sugar
1 cup chopped nuts
1 cup chocolate chips
½ tsp. soda
½ tsp. salt
1 can sweetened condensed milk

Mix together margarine, oatmeal, flour, soda, salt and brown sugar. Press into a 9 x 13 pan. On top, sprinkle chocolate chips and nuts. Over all, drizzle 1 can sweetened condensed milk. Bake about 25 minutes at 350°.

LAZY DAY STEW

Good if you want to "goof" all afternoon.

Patricia Morehead
Former State Senator, 30th District
Beatrice, NE

---

4 lbs. rump, cut in cubes
¼ cup red wine
1 can golden mushroom soup
1 can tomato sauce
1 onion, sliced
1 can mushrooms
1 green pepper, cut in rings
salt and pepper
oregano
basil

Put all in dutch oven, cover and put in 250° oven for 4½ hours.

ENERGY
IN A GLASS

This drink is a good starter in the morning. It is also a refreshing "pick me up" in the afternoon. If you are a jogger or walk for exercise, you will like to have this drink to look forward to when you're finished.

Richard Peterson, 21st District
Norfolk, NE

¼ cup mild flavored honey
1 mashed banana
½ cup unsweetened pineapple juice
1 cup cold milk
1 egg (optional)

Put all ingredients into a blender and mix until frothy.

Serve in a tall frosty glass and garnish with a wedge of orange and a maraschino cherry. If you are adventuresome, you may want to try different juices and fruits as the seasons change.

BBQ MEATBALLS

Speedy hint: use an ice cream scoop to form the balls!
R. Wiley Remmers, 1st District
Auburn, NE

13 oz. evaporated milk
3 lbs. hamburger
2 cups oatmeal
2 eggs
1 cup chopped onion
½ tsp. garlic powder
2 tsp. salt
½ tsp. pepper
2 tsp. chili powder

Mix together by hand. Use above hint to form balls. Makes about 30-40. Put topping on and bake 1 hour at 350°. Also great made smaller and served as appetizers.

Topping:
2 cups catsup
1½ cups brown sugar
2 tbsp. liquid smoke
½ cup chopped onion
½ tsp. garlic powder

LIME JELLO SALAD

My late mother, Mrs. Velma Rogers, always made this salad for holiday dinners. My wife and daughters have continued the tradition. My sons-in-law often remark that we're having "that green salad" again.

Carson Rogers, 41st District
Ord, NE

1 large package lime Jello
½ cup mayonnaise
1 small onion, chopped
2 stalks celery, diced
1 cup cottage cheese
1 green pepper, diced

Let the lime Jello set slightly and then mix in remaining ingredients and put in 9 x 11 pan and refrigerate.

FLAPJACKS

This German recipe was handed down to us from my mother's family. Great with homemade sausage on rainy days!
Stan Schellpeper, 18th District
Stanton, NE

2 cups flour
1 tsp. salt
2 well-beaten eggs
2½ cups milk
3 tbsp. shortening

Sift flour. Combine eggs, milk and shortening. Add flour and salt. Beat till smooth.

Fry as crepes. Put pat of butter in heated, round pan. Add ¾ cup of batter, tilt pan to cover bottom. Brown on one side, turn over, sprinkle liberally with sugar. Fold in half and half again. Serve hot.

May be made without butter in pan. Adjust amount of batter to size of pan.

BEEF TENDERLOIN

Since the name of our operation is Warner Hereford Farms, Inc., you will know that this recipe is best when the beef is Hereford!

Jerome Warner, 25th District
Waverly, NE

---

3 lb. beef tenderloin (trimmed by butcher)
½ stick softened butter
½ lb. mushroom caps
seasoned salt
pepper
fines herbes (Spice Island)
1½ cups good burgundy

Preheat oven to 400°. Spread butter over tenderloin; sprinkle seasoned salt, pepper (lightly) and fines herbes (lightly) over entire tenderloin. Insert meat thermometer, place tenderloin on rack in open roaster, then to the oven. At the end of 20 minutes, place mushrooms around tenderloin, then carefully pour burgundy over meat. Return to oven for about 20 minutes more, or until the desired degree of temperature. We prefer ours medium-rare, about 150° on the meat thermometer. Let roast rest about 20 minutes before slicing.

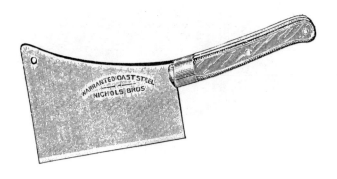

FROSTED ORANGE SALAD

A favorite from my mother since childhood...
Roger Wehrbein, 2nd District
Plattsmouth, NE

2 3-oz. packages orange gelatin
2 cups boiling water
1½ cups cold water
#2 can crushed pineapple, drained (save juice)
2-3 bananas, diced
1 cup miniature marshmallows

Dissolve gelatin in boiling water. Add cold water and chill to slightly thickened. Add drained pineapple, bananas and marshmallows. Pour into 9x13 pan. Chill until almost set.

Topping:
1 egg beaten
2 tbsp. flour
2 tbsp. butter
reserved pineapple juice plus enough water to make 1 cup liquid

Combine egg, flour, butter and pineapple juice in small saucepan. Heat and stir until thickened. Cool. Fold in 1 cup whipping cream whipped. Spread on chilled gelatin layer. If desired, spread with grated cheese. Chill about 2 hours. Makes 12 servings.

WESTERN NEBRASKA BEAN POT

Beans are one of the oldest foods known to man. Eaten with small amounts of meat or dairy products, beans supply all essential amino acids. There is NO cholesterol in beans.
John Weihing, 48th District
Gering, NE

---

1 lb. any variety of dry beans
1 ham bone or 1 cup diced ham
1 large chopped onion
6 cups water
8 oz. can green chili salsa or picante sauce

In a large pan heat washed beans in water. Boil gently for 2 minutes; turn off heat and let beans stand for 1 hour.* Then pour beans into a slow cooking pot and add remaining ingredients. Cover and cook for at least 10 hours.

* can be soaked overnight instead

DON'S DEPENDABLE DISH

Don Wesely, 26th District
Lincoln, NE

The following recipe is an old favorite of mine I developed as a bachelor first struggling through the University of Nebraska and then struggling through the Nebraska Legislature. Thank goodness I was saved from this fate by my wife whom I married in 1982. Since that time, my cooking days have all but ended. But my old favorite is always there to come to my rescue when I need an all-purpose dish for that all-important meal.

Step 1: Drive to your favorite local grocery store. There you will need to find the canned goods aisle. Here you will find those tasty treats universally beloved: Franco-American Beef Raviolio's and Chef Boyardee's Beef Ravioli. As for which brand to choose, as I am on most issues, I'm non-partisan.

Of course either ravioli comes in varying sizes. If you happen to have close friends over, I suggest the large-sized can. If you're planning a special meal just for yourself, then a smaller size will do. Having decided what size can to purchase, you then need to go to the dairy section of the grocery store and identify your favorite brand of colby cheese. Purchase these two items and head back home.

Step 2: Once home, the preparation of this dish is really quite simple. It meets my criterion of not serving a meal that takes longer to prepare than to eat. Find your favorite can opener and open your can of ravioli. Find an appropriate size saucepan for the size of the can you purchased and deposit your ravioli in the saucepan. Place the saucepan on the burner of your stove. At medium heat, warm your ravioli. While the ravioli is heating, slice up some of the colby cheese. The amount you slice up is dependent on how much you like colby cheese. When the ravioli is starting to warm, dump in the slices of cheese you cut and begin to stir the cheese into the ravioli. When the cheese is fully melted and assimilated with the ravioli, your delicious dish is ready to serve. Of course the ravioli will go well with other food you may have available. It is very flexible.

Step 3: Enjoy your food. There you have it. The special dish which carried me through college and the Legislature in my youth. It's simple, easy and inexpensive: unlike some of the Legislative issues I've been involved in. Bon appetit!

❧

WDO: As you can see, Don's recipe is quite plain and reflects something of his Legislative philosophy. In short, if you like Franco-American, you'll love Don Wesely.

Frank and Shirley Marsh at a "rotunda" (as in
Capitol Building, not physique) banquet.

Robert Spire practicing surgery (or is he sneaking nibbles?).

Bob Milligan puts
the finishing
touches on his
Seafood
Omelette.

CAPITOL COOKS AND MANSION MANAGERS

In 1963 when Kay and I moved to Nebraska, we marveled at how well-governed Nebraska was. We had just moved from Illinois, where "vote early and vote often" were the by-words and two of the last three Governors were serving time. (This may have influenced our conclusion.) We were impressed then with the hard work and dedication of Nebraska's people who served at the city, county and state levels. We still feel the same way.

BURGUNDY BURGERS

This recipe is a real winner. Even Bill says so—see below!
Allen Beerman, Secretary of State
Lincoln, NE

1½ lbs. ground chuck
1½ lbs. ground round
3 medium onions
½ cup butter
1 cup red burgundy
2 tsp. celery salt
2 tsp. dry mustard
1 tsp. salt
1 tsp. pepper
½ tsp. garlic salt
½ tsp. thyme

Saute chopped onions in butter until brown. mix with all remaining ingredients. Form into patties. Chill.

Note: For best results, cook on a griddle (flat piece of iron) instead of a grill. May use slightly less than 1 cup of burgundy depending upon moistness of the beef. Dry bread crumbs may be added to form patties and soak up the burgundy.

WDO: Allen was winner of the 1987 Celebrity Beef Cookoff at the Nebraska State Fair. (I was third.) The following year we were both entered again and I commented, "Some people might say grace BEFORE a meal—in Allen's case, one should say a prayer AFTER the meal." Whereupon, he sent me a portfolio of prayers to be said at mealtime, some of which are included in this cookbook.

59

MIXED BAKED BEANS

When you're feeding a crowd, this will be a real crowd-pleaser.
Jacquie Burt, Mansion Chef
Lincoln, NE

3 lbs. bacon ends and pieces
3 large onions
3 cups brown sugar
1½ cups vinegar (apple cider)
3 tsp. garlic salt
3 cans each (drained)
pork and beans
great northern beans
red kidney beans
large butter beans (lima)

Cut up bacon and onions in small pieces, saute and drain off grease. In very large pan or roaster, add seasoning, brown sugar, vinegar, bacon and onions. Simmer 20 minutes...very important or it will be too juicy. Turn oven on to 350°; add drained beans to mixture and cook till bubbly.

❦

WDO: Jacquie thinks my jokes are funny. That alone would qualify her as an outstanding person! What a bargain that she can cook as a professional. Whether it be for a small luncheon or a gathering of more than 100 people, Jacquie is the consumate chef. The Mansion is a happy place with well-fed people because of her.

BISMARK PANCAKES

This one will test your dexterity as well as your cooking skills.
William C. Hastings, Chief Justice
Nebraska Supreme Court
Lincoln, NE

Mix ½ cup of flour and ¾ cup of milk well.

Add a pinch of salt and 4 egg yolks and mix.

Beat whites of 4 eggs stiff and fold into the mixture.

Pour one cup of batter into well-buttered very hot skillet (6-8 inches in diameter)

When slightly brown, flip over and put into hot oven for 4 minutes.

Serve with Lingonberries or other berries of your choice, apple sauce or maple syrup.

WDO: When one looks at William Hastings, you think he ought to be a Supreme Court Justice...and he is.

SHRIMP AND TOMATO

Shot found this recipe in Playboy about four years ago and he has made it about once a month since. It's really delicious!
Candy Kleen
Deputy Director, State Dept. of Motor Vehicles
Lincoln, NE

½ lb. raw shrimp, peeled and deveined
½ lb. medium pasta shells
2 tbsp. olive oil
1 garlic clove, peeled and minced
½ cup chopped onions
1 large celery stalk, chopped
2 cups canned crushed tomatoes
¼ tsp. dried hot pepper flakes
salt and pepper
2 tbsp. minced parsley

Start water for pasta. Heat oil in skillet. Add garlic, onion and celery. Cook, stirring until soft. Add tomatoes, pepper flakes, salt and pepper to taste; stir. Bring to boil then lower heat immediately to simmer. Cook 6 to 8 minutes. Add shrimps. Cook, stirring, just until they are pink, about 2 or 3 minutes. Pour over cooked pasta and sprinkle with parsley.

GREEN PEPPER JELLY

You'll find lots of uses for this menu-enhancer. Its distinctive flavor can turn the mundane into the magnificent.
Frank and Shirley Marsh, State Treasurer
Lincoln, NE

2 cups finely ground green peppers
1 cup vinegar
1 cup water

Bring to a boil and add 1 package of Sure Jell or Pen-Gel. Bring to a full boil again then add 4 cups of sugar and ¼ tsp. salt. Boil 1 minute or until thick. Pour in glasses and seal with paraffin.

WDO: This couple has a long history of governmental involvement. Frank currently serves as State Treasurer, however he has also held the offices of Secretary of State and Lieutenant Governor. Shirley was a State Senator for many years and has now retired to become a full-time "volunteer".

HEARTY SEAFOOD OMELETTE

Serve with toast tips or bagels—
Robert S. Milligan, President, MI Industries
Lincoln, NE

8 farm fresh eggs
1 cup lowfat cottage cheese
1 cup chopped surimi crabmeat
1 diced tomato
½ cup sliced mushrooms
½ cup sliced monterey jack cheese
1 cup cheddar cheese, grated
2 tbsp. chopped chives
1 tsp. butter

Melt butter in large skillet over medium heat.

Crack eggs into mixing bowl and mix together with all other ingredients except cheddar cheese and chives. Add salt and pepper to your liking. Pour into hot skillet.

Sprinkle cheddar cheese evenly over the top of egg mixture.

Sprinkle chives over melting cheese.

Cover skillet and cook over medium heat until mixture is no longer runny. (about 10-12 minutes)

Serves 6.

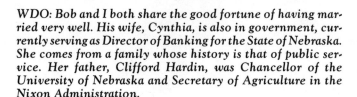

WDO: Bob and I both share the good fortune of having married very well. His wife, Cynthia, is also in government, currently serving as Director of Banking for the State of Nebraska. She comes from a family whose history is that of public service. Her father, Clifford Hardin, was Chancellor of the University of Nebraska and Secretary of Agriculture in the Nixon Administration.

ERNIE'S BBQ SAUCE MEXICANA

For any kind of meats...
Ernie Munoz, Security Officer, State Capitol
Lincoln, NE

2 cans tomato paste
1 tbsp. garlic powder
8 tbsp. BBQ sauce
¼ tsp. cumin
6 tbsp. brown sugar
3 tsp. ketchup
½ tsp. lemon juice
½ tsp. honey
1 tbsp. Gourmet wine

Combine, bring to simmer and cook 30 minutes.

WDO: Ernie has been a security guard at the State Capitol for years. When he learned I was putting out a cookbook, he commented on it. I inquired as to whether or not he was a cook. He responded that he had been since age 12 when his mother died. His brothers and sisters raised him and insisted he learn to cook as his contribution to the family. His BBQ sauce is clearly in a class by itself. After receiving a quart and using it on ribs, we decided it's as good a hot barbeque sauce as any we have ever tasted.

PETITE CHEESECAKES

These are perfect for any special occasion, but for the past few years, it's been especially important in our home that I spend several evenings about mid-December preparing enough for Joe to take to the Capitol on the day everyone in the Division brings Christmas goodies. Compliments are many. You won't mind the considerable time and patience it takes to make these little cheesecakes because they make you feel so good!

Mrs. Joe (Virginia) Neal
Lincoln, NE

---

3 8 oz. packages cream cheese
5 eggs
1½ cups sugar
3 cups sour cream
vanilla
2 cans cherry pie filling

Cream together softened cheese with 1 cup sugar. Add 2 tsp. vanilla. Add 5 eggs one at a time, beating each in thoroughly. Pour this mixture into cupcake papers set in muffin tins. Fill cups ½ full (cups 1¾" diameter). Bake at 350° for 25 minutes.

Meanwhile, mix 3 cups sour cream with ½ cup sugar and 2 tsp. vanilla. Remove muffin pans from oven. The cakes will "fall" (sink in) a bit. Nothing is wrong, they are supposed to do this. Spoon about 1½ tsps. of this mixture on each cake. Put a cherry (from can of pie filling) on each cake. Return to oven and bake for another 10 minutes.

If you need to remove the cakes from the muffin pans while they are still hot, use tweezers to lift cakes out of pans. Cool and refrigerate. Can also be frozen and used at a later date.

❧

WDO: This Joe Neal is Director of Security at the State Capitol. His wife, Virginia, is an Administrative Assistant for Investment Operations at Woodmen Accident and Life. Another "across the street from each other" working couple like us!

BRUNCH
CHEESE-EGG BAKE

Make this on Saturday night and serve your whole family Sunday morning. This is great for Christmas morning...also for a luncheon dish using tuna, shrimp or turkey for the meat.
Mrs Bill (Ruth) Nichol, Wife of Lt. Governor
Scottsbluff, NE

Grease bottom of 9x13x2 cake pan. Cover bottom with one layer of 6 slices white bread, cut diagonally. Top with 10 oz. of sharp cheddar cheese sliced. Add 2 cups crumbled bacon, sausage or diced ham. Beat 6 eggs, 3½ cups of milk, 2¼ tsp. salt, ¾ tsp. prepared mustard, 1½ tbsp. Worcestershire sauce. Place 6 more slices of bread cut diagonally over top and pour milk mixture slowly over all. Let stand overnight and bake at 325° for 1 hour or until knife comes out clean.

WDO: Bill was Kay's running mate. His campaign efforts helped make for a successful result.

AUNT PEG'S FRIED TURKEY BITS

No these AREN'T "turkey fries"...they're "fried turkeys" and they're terrific.

Jack Peetz, Attorney
Lincoln, NE

Cut breast and thighs of a turkey into 1″ squares x ½″ thick pieces...

Soak squares in a covered plastic container of milk in refrigerator for 24 hours...

Put flour, salt, pepper and paprika in a plastic bag...

Place 5-6 squares in seasoning bag and shake till covered...

Preheat electric skillet to 325-350°; use oleo for frying...

Add seasoned bits and fry until golden brown on both sides.

WDO: Jack met Natalie Cross while she was the Governor's representative in Western Nebraska. Until that time, Jack was a confirmed bachelor and no one in Sidney thought he would ever get married. Natalie had other plans for him and her name is now Natalie Cross Peetz. (Welcome to the Governor's office "family", Jack!)

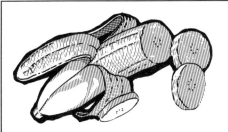

CAPIROTADA

That's "Mexican Bread Pudding" to those of you not familiar with Mexican menu items beyond tacos or nachos.

Joe Ruis, Nebraska State Patrol
Governor's Security Force
Lincoln, NE

2 cups water
1½ cups brown sugar (packed)
¾ tsp. ground cinnamon
4 cinnamon sticks
8-12 slices bread
2 tbsp. butter or margarine
½ cup raisins
¾ cup almond slices
2 medium bananas, sliced
¾ cup cheese, shredded

In medium saucepan combine water, brown sugar, ground cinnamon, cinnamon sticks and bring to a boil. Reduce heat and let simmer uncovered 2-3 minutes. Stir in butter.

In medium size dutch oven, layer bread, raisins, cheese, bananas, almond slices and cinnamon sticks. Pour sugar mixture over individual layers.

Cover and bake in preheated 350° oven for 40 minutes. Serve warm. May be served with cream if so desired.

WDO: Joe and his mother represent some of the best of Hispanic cooking in Nebraska. They do this as a sideline and Joe contends his recipes are as good as any—in or out of professional restaurants.

GREAT CHICKEN

This recipe is shared with me by Jerre Van Steenberg of Scotts-bluff.

Mrs. Robert (Elaine) Spire, Wife of Attorney General
State of Nebraska, Lincoln, NE

Skin 3 lb. chicken or chicken pieces
Mix together:
1 bottle Russian dressing (8 oz.)
1 envelope dry onion soup mix
1 cup orange marmalade

Brush chicken all over; marinate overnight.

Bake at 350° for 45 minutes, turn over, bake 15 more minutes. Serves 4 to 6.

❧

WDO: Bob's legal expertise would not be worth much if it were not for his ability to play the piano. The latter is more than enough to offset the former. Given that, we accept his (her?) recipe with grace and the hope that it is every bit as good as his legal/musical abilities.

DATE CHOCOLATE CHIP CAKE

An unexpected combination results in an elegant "special" dessert.

Karen Toussaint, Mansion Manager
Lincoln, NE

---

1 cup dates cut up small
1 tsp. soda

Pour 1½ cups boiling water over above and let stand.
Cream 1 cup sugar with 1 cup margarine.
Add 2 eggs, 2 cups flour and 1 tsp. soda (in addition to above).
Pour date mixture over and blend.
Pour into 9 x 13 cake pan—greased and floured.

TOPPING:
½ cup sugar
1 cup chopped pecans
6 oz. package chocolate chips

Sprinkle over top of cake; bake at 350° for 35-40 minutes.
Serve topped with whipped cream.

WDO: Karen is the person who makes it all "go together". She manages the equivalent of a small hotel and the staff that goes with it, with a flair and enthusiasm that cause many to wonder where Karen gets her boundless energy. Her help with the cookbook was invaluable.

SHRIMP, MUSHROOM AND ARTICHOKE CASSEROLE

This is better if made the day before you want to serve it.
Cathy Tverstol, Volunteer, Governor's Office
Lincoln, NE

2 ½ tbsp. butter
½ lb. mushrooms
1½ lbs. shrimp
#2 can of artichokes
4 ½ tbsp. butter
4 ½ tbsp. flour
¾ cup milk
¾ cup whipping cream
½ cup dry sherry
1 tbsp. Worcestershire sauce
salt and pepper to taste
½ cup Parmesan cheese
paprika

Melt 2½ tbsp. butter and saute mushrooms. Set aside. Boil and shell shrimp. In a 2 qt. casserole, make one layer each of artichoke hearts, shrimp and mushrooms.

To make sauce: melt 4½ tbsp. butter. Stirring with a wire whisk, add the flour, then the milk and cream. Stir until thick. Add sherry, Worcestershire, salt and pepper. Pour over layered ingredients. Sprinkle top with cheese and paprika. Bake in 375° oven for 20-30 minutes. Serve over rice. Serves 6.

❧

WDO: Cathy is a "volunteer" in Kay's office. She is so good as a volunteer, some think she is a full-time professional. Must be she enjoys being in the eye of the hurricane.

RESPECTABLE REPUBLICANS

Is there another kind? Since this is a bipartisan cookbook (or should we say nonpartisan?) perhaps this chapter distinguishing GOP gastronomes was not necessary—but here it is anyway.

BAKED ARTICHOKE DIP

Mrs. Duane (Phyllis) Acklie
Lincoln, NE

1 cup sour cream
1 cup mayonnaise
1 can artichokes (not marinated!)
1 cup Parmesan cheese
½ cup green onion, chopped fine
dash of beau monde seasoning
dash of garlic powder

Bake at 350° for 20 minutes. Serve with Cheddar Thins crackers.

HOMEMADE
ICE CREAM

Duane Acklie, President
Crete Carriers, Lincoln, NE

(Using 1½ gallon freezer)
6 eggs
3 cups sugar
1 tbsp. vanilla
½ tsp. salt (or slightly less)

Beat eggs well. Add sugar slowly; add vanilla and salt. Gradually add milk (or half and half or cream, depending on your likeness of richness!). Fill freezer to within 2 inches of top. Use plenty of rock salt sprinkled through ice while freezing. Crank or plug in and enjoy.

CHOCOLATE GOOP

Duane Acklie, President
Crete Carriers, Lincoln, NE

¾ of a 2 lb. can of Nestle's Quik
½ cup water to moisten
1 bottle clear Karo syrup

Mix chocolate with water until dissolved. Add syrup. Heat over medium heat just until very hot. Don't boil. Serve over ice cream.

WDO: Duane has never been known for his prowess as a chef, but rather for taking a small trucking company to one of national importance. The best thing he's ever done was marry Phyllis—she's the real secret to his success.

SEAFOOD
EN PAPILLOTE

The Epicurean Restaurant in Columbia, South Carolina uses a version of this recipe as a first course—served in individual parchment envelopes.

Bill and Shari Apking
Former Mayor, Alexandria, NE

---

1 lb. cod fillets (or other similar white fish)
¼ lb. peeled and deveined medium shrimp
meat from 2 or 3 large crab legs
½ lb. scallops
meat from 1 medium lobster tail (optional)
2 lg. white onions, sliced
4 tbsp. white wine
1½ tbsp. oregano
pepper

Line 2 qt. casserole with sheet of cooking parchment, leaving enough above rim to cover filled dish. Cut cod fillets, crab, and lobster into manageable pieces. Mix seafood together and place in casserole, sprinkle with wine, pepper and 1 tbsp. oregano. Top with sliced onions. Sprinkle additional ½ tbsp. oregano over onions. Pin parchment shut, then cover with lid. Bake at 325° for 45 minutes. Serves 4.

WDO: The Apkings are among our friends from Young Republican days. It is not difficult to get an opinion from Bill. Fortunately, he was also willing to share this recipe, which his wife calls his "piece de resistance".

ZESTY CARROTS

We first ate this dish at a restored Shaker village in Kentucky. Obviously they expected people to enjoy it, because they had copies of the recipe ready to hand out to those who asked for it.
Dennis and Charlyne Berens
Editor/Publisher, Seward (NE) County Independent

6-8 carrots, pared and cut lengthwise
2 tbsp. horseradish
2 tbsp. grated onion
½ tsp. salt
1 tbsp. melted butter
½ cup mayonnaise
¼ cup fine bread or cracker crumbs
¼ tsp. pepper
dash of paprika

Cook carrots in a little water until tender. Reserve ¼ cup of cooking liquid. Arrange carrots in a shallow baking dish. Combine horseradish, onion, carrot liquid, salt, pepper and mayo. Pour over carrots. Combine crumbs, butter and paprika; sprinkle over top. Bake 15-20 minutes at 375°. Add extra baking time if chilled. Serves 6.

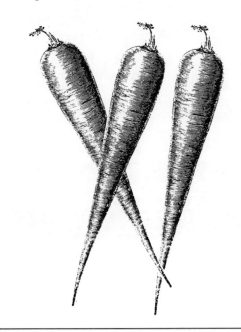

PISTACHIO SALAD

Mrs. Dwight Burney, Former First Lady
State of Nebraska
Polk, NE

3 oz. package instant pistachio pudding
9 oz. carton whipped topping
15 oz. marshmallows
½ cup chopped walnuts

Make pudding mix according to directions on package. Mix in other ingredients and refrigerate overnight.

MILK TOAST

I credit this recipe with carrying me through nine campaigns and through half a century of law practice with more than my share of hard fought trials. Even now, it allows me, a late sep-tuagenerian, to enjoy an hour and a half of serious tennis two days each week.

Robert Crosby—Former Governor, State of Nebraska
Lincoln, NE

Pour a cup of whole milk in a cooking receptacle, prefera-bly an old aluminum pan. Place on the small burner on the range with low heat. Do not allow to reach a boil – it will be hard enough to scrape the inside of the pan anyway.

When the milk is close to a boil, carefully break two eggs into the milk.

While the eggs are slowly cooking in the milk, place two slices of nutritious bread in the toaster. The toast should be golden brown.

Take one large dinner plate and place the pieces of toast side by side on the plate.

Put two large cuts of butter (margarine if you insist) in the hot milk. When the butter is about half melted, carefully pour the hot milk with the eggs and the butter on the two slices of toast. Salt and pepper to one's taste.

The above dinner is guaranteed to induce sound sleep, per-mitting one to feel rested and ready for the next day's activities.

WDO: Better make sure the dinner plate has a pretty high rim around it if you don't want to have to cry over spilled milk! By the way, he isn't kidding about the tennis. He's a determined player despite arthritis in both hips.

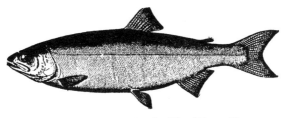

SPICY BAR-B-Q
SALMON

Hint: Save all your bacon fat for this!
Carl T. Curtis, U.S. Senator (retired)
Lincoln, NE

Slice:
8 to 12 fillets of salmon—leave skin on.
Spread in a single layer, skin down, in a long, deep pan.

In a large bowl, mix:
3 cups brown sugar
1 cup coarse or rock salt
1 tsp. nutmeg
1 tsp. cinnamon
1 tsp. garlic powder
½ tsp. ground cloves

Spread evenly over salmon fillets. Gently add just enough water to cover fish; let stand 5 to 6 hours. Occasionally, stir and spoon sugar mixture up over fish.

Final preparation:

Light your barbeque coals, drain fish, but try to leave fairly thick coating of the sugar glaze on fillets.

Melt:

Lots of bacon fat (½ cup or so). Brush thickly over both sides of fillets. SLOWLY barbeque fillets, meat side down (facing coals). Remove when slightly undercooked (takes 5-10 minutes) and when you are ready to serve, finish cooking in hot oven. This saves you fussing over "hot coals" while guests wait at the table!

Serves 8 to 12.

❧

WDO: Carl's record of public service in Congress is well known. Perhaps not so well known, but equally impressive, are his culinary abilities. He is also as busy in "retirement" as most people are during their active careers.

SANDHILL TROUT BAKED ON ORANGE WILD RICE

One might think it is risky business for a lawyer in cattle country to suggest fish, but, in truth, an easy truce prevails. Trout fishing is as accepted a Sandhills sport as is turkey and grouse hunting. The ranchers who own the streams know an occasional creel of wild trout will never be sufficient to supplant filet (as in beef) with fillet (as in fish) as the protein staple of our western palate. While this recipe is not original...I offer it without guilt of plagiarism, knowing that the genius who created it was undoubtedly a trout connoisseur who would want us all to enjoy the very best in "fin" cuisine.

John A. Gale, Former State Chairman
Nebraska Republican Party
North Platte, NE

---

2 cups wild rice, rinsed well and drained
1½ tsp. salt
¾ stick (6 tbsp.) unsalted butter
1 large bunch of scallions, chopped
(reserve ¼ cup of green part for garnish)
6¾ lb. brook trout, cleaned and boned
(keep heads and tails intact)
½ lemon, cut into 6 wedges
1 cup fresh orange juice
2 tsp. grated orange rind
6 thin slices of orange and 6 parsley sprigs for garnish

In a saucepan, combine the wild rice with the salt and 6 cups cold water. Bring to a boil, simmer for 35-45 minutes until rice is just tender. Drain, toss with 3 tbsp. softened butter and scallions. Spread wild rice evenly in a buttered large shallow baking dish. Cut remaining 3 tbsp. butter into 6 slices. Season cavities of the trout with salt and pepper and stuff each cavity with a wedge of lemon and 1 slice of butter. Arrange trout on top of rice, pour orange juice over them, bake covered with buttered wax paper and foil, in a preheated oven at 400° for 30 minutes, or until trout just flakes. Sprinkle the wild rice with the reserved ¼ cup scallions and orange rind, garnish each trout with a twist of sliced orange and a parsley sprig. Serves 6.

❦

WDO: A friend of long-standing, John is a Former State Chairman of the Nebraska Republican Party. He is fearless as you can tell by the courage of his recipe submission—fish—from the Sandhills country where beef is king.

FRED'S FAVORITE ORIENTAL BBQ RIBS

A slightly different approach to a very popular item...
Fred Hawkins, Jr., President
Hawkins Construction Company
Omaha, NE

4 pounds pork back ribs
garlic salt to taste
⅓ cup hoisin sauce
⅓ cup soy sauce
⅓ cup brown sugar
⅓ cup sugar
2 tbsp. white wine

Place ribs in large roasting pan and sprinkle with garlic salt. Cover the pan with foil and roast in a 350° oven for one hour. Drain off the fat and cut meat into individual rib segments. Combine the remaining ingredients in a small bowl and pour over the ribs. Marinate for a least 2 hours, turning occasionally. Brown on the grill and serve immediately. Serves 4.

WDO: Fred and Marianne are proof that one-plus-one can equal almost anything they decide to equal. Omaha and Nebraska are better because of them.

PASTA WITH ZUCCHINI

Yet another way to use up the prolific products of a summer garden!

Mike Heavican, Lancaster County Attorney
Lincoln, NE

½ cup oil
2 medium onions, chopped
2 cloves of garlic, chopped
1 pound of zucchini, chopped
2 medium green peppers, chopped
4 fresh tomatoes, chopped
salt to taste
1/8 tsp. pepper

Heat oil in large skillet. Add onions, garlic, zucchini and peppers; saute 5 minutes. Add tomatoes, salt and pepper; cook over low heat 5 minutes or until vegetables are crisp-tender. Use over pasta. That's it!

WDO: Mike says this mixture can be combined with ground beef if you like. Sounds plenty good to me just the way it is...maybe with a nice medium-rare T-bone on the "side" and a glass of Cabernet Sauvignon?

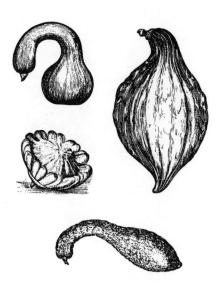

THOUSAND ISLAND DRESSING

I have shared this recipe more times than any others I have.
Gwen Hersberger
Milford, NE

---

1 cup mayonnaise or salad dressing
½ cup sugar
¼ cup catsup
½ tsp. celery seed
¼ cup pickle relish
½ tsp. Worcestershire sauce
2 hard-boiled eggs, grated
salt and pepper

Combine above ingredients and refrigerate.

WDO: Gwen is the epitome of enthusiasm, no matter what she's doing: raising horses, supporting Republican politics, cooking or providing leadership in her community.

BAKED FISH

A good way to cook a really good piece of fish. Simple and not so seasoned as to overwhelm the natural flavor of the fillets.
Mrs. Roman (Victoria) Hruska
Wife of U.S. Senator (retired)
Omaha, NE

---

3 or 4 fish fillets
rolled cracker crumbs
¼ lb. melted butter or oleo
mayonnaise

Spread dried fillets with mayonnaise; roll in crumbs. Place in shallow pan which has butter melted in the bottom.

Bake in hot—400°— oven for 20 minutes or until nicely browned. No need to turn fish.

WDO: Roman and Vickie continue to contribute to the welfare of Nebraska, as they did the State and Nation during the time they lived in Washington, D.C.

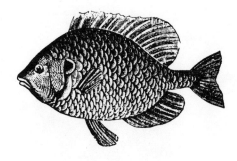

HIDDEN VALLEY
HOT POTATO SALAD

A change of pace from the more traditional hot German-style potato salad. Fast and easy, too.
Dave and Liz Karnes, Former U.S. Senator
Omaha, NE

2 lbs. small red new potatoes, cooked and unpeeled
½ cup sliced red onions
1 cup prepared Hidden Valley Ranch
with Bacon dressing
paprika
black pepper
chives

While still warm, cut potatoes into 1″ cubes. Gently toss with onions and salad dressing. Dust with paprika and black pepper. Garnish with fresh chives. Serve warm.

❦

WDO: When Senator Zorinsky died in February of 1987, Governor Orr appointed Dave Karnes United States Senator from Omaha. He served with distinction, while at the same time making himself known to Nebraskans throughout the state. He and Liz gave an outstanding effort to the U.S. Senate race in the fall of 1988.

SALMON PATE

Delicious to use as an hors d'oeuvre with your favorite mild crackers.

Joan and Bob Kayton
Cedar Rapids, NE

½ cup hot water
1 tbsp. gelatin
1 tbsp. chicken boullion
1 can salmon
4 shallots
¼ cup mayonnaise
2 tsp. lemon juice
salt and pepper
½ cup cream

Pour hot water, gelatin and chicken broth in blender. Blend at high speed one minute.

Add undrained salmon, shallots and lemon juice. Blend one minute.

Add cream, blend 30 seconds.

Pour into mold. Chill.

WDO: A couple of real community leaders—literally. Also staunch Republicans and friends who enjoy cooking.

PORK SAUSAGE CASSEROLE

You know any pork recipe submitted by a cattle rancher has to be good!

Ralph J. Knobel, Former Chairman
Nebraska Republican Party
Fairbury, NE

---

1 cup water
½ cup rice
¼ tsp. salt
Cook together on low heat until rice is tender.
1 lb. seasoned pork sausage
¼ cup minced onion
½ cup chopped celery
¼ cup chopped green pepper or pimento (or mixed)
1 can cream of mushroom soup
¼ cup water

Brown sausage and onion together in heavy skillet. In 2-quart casserole dish, mix rice, sausage, chopped celery and green pepper/pimento. Combine the mushroom soup and milk and add to the other ingredients. Bake in 350⁰ oven for 30 minutes or until well heated.

WDO: Ralph is one of the state's most successful farmers. To be frank, he knows less about cooking than he does about eating. The fact that he married an outstanding cook is what really makes it worthwhile to visit Ralph and his family.

FRIED CABBAGE

Art is not a cook, but he loves good food. I'm sure that makes him an expert. This is a specialty at our house...it makes my mouth water just to think about it.

Mrs. Art (Earlene) Knox
Wife of Sr. Vice President, Commerce Capital, Inc.
Lincoln, NE

1 large head of cabbage
cooking oil
1 cup water
½ cup half and half
2 tsp. vinegar
salt to taste

Shred cabbage very coarsely. Heat oil in frying pan and add cabbage. Pour on water, cover and let it steam. Stir often. When well-steamed, remove cover and let the cabbage brown and cook down. When nicely browned, add cream and vinegar. Stir well and cook short time longer.

WDO: Long-time Republican and church friends, Art and Earlene suffered a major house fire some time back. I'm sure glad no one was hurt and their recipes weren't destroyed!

INDIVIDUAL BAKED NEBRASKA

Ed. Note: We renamed his recipe which was originally submitted as Individual Baked Alaska. Apologies to our friends up North...

Roland Langemeier
Schuyler, NE

Makes 4 servings

Place ½" thick slices of angel food cake on a cookie sheet.

Top with generous scoop of ice cream.

Place in deep freeze for two hours.

Topping:

Beat 3 egg whites until frothy—adding 6 tbsp. of sugar and ½ tsp. vanilla.

Frost ice cream and cake pieces.

Place in preheated oven (475-500°) for 2-3 minutes or until light brown.

Serve immediately!

WDO: I've never had the nerve to try this, but if Roland can do it, so can I. (Still think I'll use a cookie sheet with edges just in case...)

GOOSEBERRY JAM

Picking the berries can be painful because of the thorns, but the jam is worth the effort!

John Lowe
Kearney, NE

1 quart gooseberries
½ cup water
4 cups sugar
1 package Sure Jell (1¾ oz.)

Remove stems and blossoms from berries. Place berries in colander and mash; then put berries in saucepan and add water. Heat to boiling and stir. Add sugar. Boil preserves quickly until berries are clear and the juice is thick, about 15 minutes. Add Sure Jell.

WDO: Lowe notes there aren't very many gooseberry bushes in Nebraska, but the ones that are were planted by Leprechauns in the dark of the night. According to him, the little people followed the Irish immigrants to our state and at night they would sneak out and plant gooseberries, planning to follow the trail of green bushes later to find their way back to Ireland. Assuming this jam is as good as the story that goes with it, we've got a winner.

OPEN FACE
TUNA MELTS

A hot sandwich that is good-looking, good-tasting and good for you.

Roland A. Luedtke, Attorney
Lincoln, NE

6½ oz. can of tuna, drained and flaked
Miracle Whip salad dressing
2 tbsp. finely chopped celery
2 tbsp. finely chopped carrot
2 tbsp. finely chopped onion
dash of pepper
2 English muffins, split and toasted
4 Velveeta slices, cut in half diagonally

Combine tuna, ¼ cup salad dressing, vegetables and pepper. Mix lightly. Spread muffin halves with additional salad dressing. Cover with tuna mixture and top with cheese slices. Broil until cheese begins to melt. Makes 4 sandwiches.

WDO: Roland has been Lt. Governor of Nebraska and Mayor of Lincoln. Despite all of these activities, he has learned more about tuna than Johnny Carson. (See page 179.)

PINE TREE
GULCH GRILLED
STEAK

This steak was served with fried potatoes at the Luff cabin for many years. Each time, the comment was, "The best I ever tasted!". Kay and Bill Orr are among the many who have enjoyed it.

Earl T. Luff, Retired Chairman, Lincoln Steel
Lincoln, NE

Have steaks cut ¾ to 1 inch thick (thicker if you prefer) from your favorite cut of beef. If thicker steaks are used, more careful and slower grilling will be necessary to get the desired results. Be sure steaks are at room temperature and baste liberally with basting sauce about 30 minutes before grilling begins.

First sear the steaks briefly on both sides and then begin the grilling and basting. Turn the steaks only once while grilling and be careful not to puncture them with a fork or other sharp utensil. Baste to taste with the sauce shown below:

1 cup peanut or corn oil
1 cup wine vinegar
1 large onion grated
1 tsp. salt
1 tsp. black pepper, freshly ground or crushed
4 rather thin slices from garlic clove

Place all ingredients in a covered jar and shake vigorously. Let stand 12 to 24 hours before using.

For variation, add either one or both of the following:
1 tbsp. dry mustard, 2 tbsp. Worcestershire sauce.

For Teriyaki Steak:
Omit wine vinegar; add 1 cup soy sauce and 1 tbsp. brown sugar.

Basting sauce may also be used as a marinade. Store in refrigerator.

❦

WDO: How can one describe a man who has done so much for so many for so long?

CALICO SALAD

Different and very good—Kay will love it.
Inez Mock, Former Republican Chair
Boone County, NE

Cook 6 to 8 minutes and cool:
16 oz. package frozen mixed vegetables
small package frozen lima beans

Add:
¼ cup chopped onion
½ cup chopped celery
½ cup chopped green pepper

Mix: 1 package Hidden Valley dressing and 1 cup mayonnaise.

Pour over vegetables, marinate overnight and serve.

WDO: I would've included this one just because of the name...but it also sounds good, and I like anything that can be done way ahead of time without damage to itself or those who consume it.

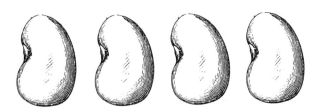

DRY MIX BBQ SALT

This may be made in any quantities you want, as it stores well. It was acquired from my friend Travis Eckert, who is known as the Barbeque King of Austin, Texas.
Paul Mohr, Owner, Ideal Laundry
Scottsbluff, NE

5 tbsp. salt
1½ tbsp. red pepper
2 tbsp. black pepper
½ tbsp. garlic salt
1 tbsp. paprika
1 tbsp. allspice

WDO: Paul didn't send along any "preferences" for what he likes to sprinkle this on when grilling. Sounds to me like it'd give a little "zip" to just about anything you can cook over charcoal.

CHICKEN DIABLE

A beautiful and tasty glaze makes this chicken entree special.
Morris and Joanie Ochsner
Republican Chairman
Madison County, NE

1 broiler/fryer, cut up (about 3 lbs.)
½ cup honey
¼ cup prepared mustard
1 tsp. curry powder
4 tbsp. butter or margarine
1 tsp. salt

Wash chicken pieces, pat dry; remove skin if you wish. Melt butter or margarine in a shallow baking pan; stir in remaining ingredients. Roll chicken pieces in butter mixture to coat both sides, then arrange, meaty side up in a single layer in same pan. Bake in moderate oven (375⁰) one hour or until chicken is tender and richly glazed. (350⁰ if using glass pan.)

❧

WDO: The definition of "Republican" has to include these two people.

JO'S SPAGHETTI SAUCE

This is one of those "by guess and by golly" recipes. You can improvise, if necessary. In the state shown below, it is a favorite at our house...even better the second day.
John Payne, Board of Regents
University of Nebraska
Kearney, NE

---

3 lbs. hamburger, browned and drained
1 package Italian sausage, browned and drained
1 double package powdered spaghetti sauce mix
diced onion and green pepper to preference
2 cans tomato soup
1 can tomato sauce
1 can tomato puree or paste
1 can stewed tomatoes (optional)
shredded American and/or cheddar cheese (to taste)

After browning and draining meats, add remaining ingredients and simmer for at least 2 hours. Makes a big potful.

WDO: John and his wife Jodelle (as in Jo's Spaghetti Sauce) are loyal Republican supporters and prominent citizens of Kearney. You can tell by the title of this recipe who is the cook in their household.

EISENHOWER DRESSING

*This recipe is so titled not because we think Ike had a fond-
ness for it, but because it was swapped among a group of us who
served in the Eisenhower Administration in Washington, D.C.
in the 50's.*

Dean Pohlenz, Debonnaire Wordsmith (retired)
Lincoln, NE

3 oz. cream cheese, softened
½ cup crumbled blue cheese
½ cup salad dressing
½ cup light cream
1 tbsp. lemon juice

Blend all ingredients. Makes 1½ cups.

*WDO: How does one write well about someone who writes
well? Well...?*

HOMEMADE ICE CREAM

Simple ingredients, uncomplicated instructions and tastes great!

Ralph Schmadeke, Schmadeke Inc.
Albion, NE

Beat together:
6 eggs
1¾ cup sugar
1 qt. cream
2 tsp. vanilla
1 tsp. lemon juice
dash of salt

Pour in gallon freezer, add whole milk to fill up to 1 inch from top of freezer. Use crank or electric freezer and plenty of ice cream freezer salt. For variations use crushed pineapple or chocolate syrup.

WDO: Albion, Nebraska is one of the most upbeat communities in the state and Ralph Schmadeke and his mother are two of the reasons why.

OLD FASHIONED FARM STYLE TOMATO SOUP

Secret recipe of three generations of the Schuetz family...it was a daily meal while growing up on the farm as a young boy. Still in later years, at least once a week, a bowl of tomato soup is a must.

Jack Schuetz, JSHA, Inc.
Lincoln, NE

---

1 pint home grown ripe tomatoes canned
(pressure cooker or water bath)
1 pint whole milk or 2% milk
1/8 to ¼ tsp. baking soda
salt and pepper to taste

With egg beater, beat 1 pint canned tomatoes until smooth. Place in large pan. Place milk in another large pan. Place both pans on stove on high heat. When milk comes to boil, turn down heat to low. When tomato pulp comes to boil, turn down heat to medium. Add baking soda to tomatoes. It will foam up. Reduce heat and stir into warm milk slowly. If milk curdles a little, it is because not enough baking soda was used. Take egg beater and beat until curds disappear. Ladle into large soup bowls, salt and pepper to taste, garnish with a sprig of parsley. Serves 4.

If home grown canned tomatoes are not available, substitute canned tomatoes purchased from store. Fresh peeled tomatoes cooked, can also be used.

WDO: Jack has been "Mr. Republican" for many years. Most people feel they have not attended a GOP gathering until they see Jack with his hat and coat adorned with stickers, buttons, badges and various identification indicating Jack is "uncommitted". What a NICE guy...

TOSSED SALAD DRESSING

Use olive oil in this...it's good for your heart. Your skin, too.
Pat (Mrs. Richard) Smith
Former National GOP Committee Woman
Lincoln, NE

1 tsp. salt
½ tsp. dry mustard
¼ tsp. medium grind black pepper
¼ tsp. paprika

Blend and add:
7 tbsp. no-cholesterol oil
3 tbsp. Spice Islands red vinegar with garlic
juice of ½ lemon

WDO: In 1964, Pat encouraged Kay to get involved in politics. We call her the "Godmother" since she was responsible for getting Kay involved as a "volunteer". The truth is, without Pat Smith, Kay would probably not be Governor of the State of Nebraska. (I'll never forgive her.)

LAW AND ORDER SPAGHETTI SAUCE

What else could I name it? No one can spell or say Staskiewicz's Spaghetti Sauce!
Ronald L. Staskiewicz, Douglas County Attorney
Omaha, NE

2 (1 lb. 1 oz.) cans whole tomatoes
2 (8 oz.) cans tomato paste
1 medium white onion, diced
1 large clove garlic, minced
1 large green pepper, diced
2 tbsp. olive oil
1½ lb. hot Italian sausage
1 lb. extra lean ground round formed into meatballs
2 tbsp. brown sugar
1 dash red pepper seeds
3 bay leaves, crushed thoroughly
salt to taste
2 tbsp. black pepper
1 tsp. garlic salt
1 tsp. onion salt
2 tbsp. red wine
1 egg
Italian seasoning (purchased as one spice)

Saute in olive oil the minced garlic, diced onion and diced green pepper all together until they are soft. (Approximately 15 minutes at medium heat.)

Add whole tomatoes (cut) and tomato paste (this thickens the sauce). Add brown sugar to enhance the flavor of the sauce. Add Italian seasoning, garlic salt, onion salt, red pepper seeds, bay leaves, red wine, black pepper and salt to taste. Add sauteed mixture of garlic, onions and peppers.

In a separate pan, cook sausage thoroughly. Make meatballs with a touch of Italian spice, salt, pepper and the beaten egg. Fry until medium-cooked. Place meat in sauce and let simmer for a minimum of 6 hours. The longer the better as simmering will reduce the acidity in the tomatoes.

The sauce is now ready to be used on your favorite spaghetti. Enjoy!

❧

WDO: Ron has had a great positive influence on law enforcement in the Omaha area. I like the way he's included "educational" comments in his recipe. Helps neophyte chefs understand the chemistry of it all.

ANGEL FOOD CAKE

For years, this recipe came out of the cake flour box. Now, I think it's committed to memory.

Charles Thone, Former Governor
State of Nebraska
Lincoln, NE

Separate 12 eggs at room temperature
(should make about 1 ½ cups of whites)

Add to whites:
1½ tsp. cream of tartar
¼ tsp. salt
1 tsp. vanilla
½ tsp. almond flavoring

Sift 1 cup of cake flour with ¾ cup of sugar 4 times.

Beat whites at low speed to mix flavorings, then at high until stiff, yet moist.

At low speed, blend in ¾ cup sugar with mixer. By hand, fold in flour mixture (folding counterclockwise by fourths of bowl, a small amount at a time).

Gently push batter into very clean angel food pan; slowly slice butter knife through mixture to settle air bubbles.

Bake at 375° for 30 to 35 minutes. Listen to cake to test for doneness. If it's still making sounds, put back in oven for about 5 minutes. Cool upside down.

The best frosting to retain the cake's flavor is simply softened butter, powdered sugar, cap of vanilla and enough whole milk to make it spreadable.

WDO: Charlie Thone is a practicing attorney. However, he was also Governor of Nebraska and a United States Congressman. He appointed Kay as his Chief of Staff and gave her a first-hand view of the Governor's Office. She must have liked it.

A LILAC FARM CHILI SUPPER FOR SIX

Lourene Wishart, Longtime GOP Lady
Lincoln, NE

---

1 egg size Lilac Farm grown bermuda onion,
peeled and chopped
1½ lbs. lean ground sirloin steak
2 tbsp. Lilac Farm smoked champion
ham/bacon drippings
or
fry 3 strips smokey bacon and use the drippings
1 qt. homemade Lilac Farm grown
"Sioux" tomato juice*
2 or 3 cans Richlieu red kidney beans*
French's chili powder to taste

Saute onion in drippings 3-4 minutes. Remove. Add ground sirloin and fry slowly until brown. Return the onions and mix in all the other ingredients and cook slowly until chili powder and all are well blended.

To be sure of NO scorch, place in a double boiler and let simmer until needed. Serve in deep soup plates with warmed crackers.

A dutch oven type of deep iron or aluminum cooking utensil is desirable, but not necessary.

* depends on quantity preferred and thickness desired

WDO: Lourene also sent in a poem and a song about the GOP, but here we only include her recipe.

RESERVED

......for those whose political philosophy is in between The Respectable Republicans and The Decent Democrats — as is this page. If your views lie outside either of these partisan parameters, this page may be used for your favorite independent or third party recipe. (I collect party recipes; please send me a copy.)

WDO

DECENT DEMOCRATS

There is only one person in this chapter. Does this mean there is only one Decent Democrat in Nebraska or the United States? Well — no — but the fact is, Roger Welsch is a "Democrat" and quite decent at the same time. Most importantly, he is in a class by himself and thus we designate him as THE Decent Democrat.

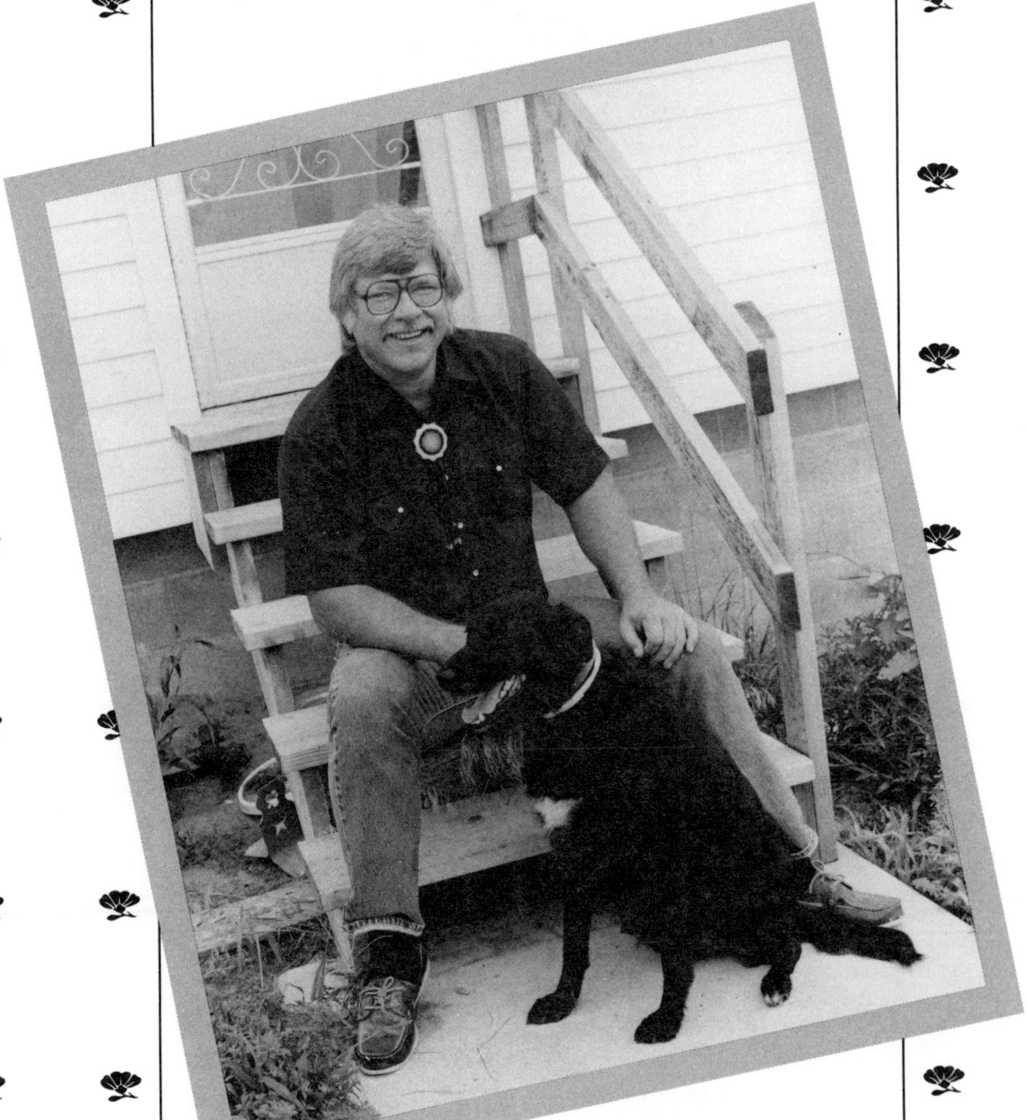

ROGER'S GIN-AND-TONIC DISSERTATION

Roger Welsch, Author/Entertainer
Dannebrog, NE

Linda loves whatever I cook, not so much because I am such a GREAT cook, but because when I cook, SHE doesn't have to cook. When I cook, I always cook over an open fire, summer and winter, grill, smoker, campfire and fireplace. I smoke fish and fowl, prefer shishkabobs and steaks on the grill (turn them only once!), and that sort of thing, but the most important ingredient for all of my cooking, the true secret of my considerable culinary eclat (well, YOU wrote to me!) is the gin-and-tonics I drink while I cook.

Far too little credit is given the gin-and-tonic. It was invented by the English during their colonial period in Africa and Asia and accounts in large part for the longevity and power of the little country of England for so long.

The tonic water provided the quinine that stilled the ague of malaria; the slice of lime thwarted the scurvy that cursed the English sailor—or "limey" as he came to be called, and the gin purified the often contaminated water. A gin-and-tonic is a little like a medicine chest. Look at me: strong as an ox.

But a gin-and-tonic must be made right, and it rarely is. The very best plan is to start with tonic-water ice cubes. The most obvious problem with keeping a tray of tonic-water ice cubes, however, is the constant danger of some kid dropping one in the Kool-Aid. Tastes terrible.

If you don't have tonic water ice cubes, freeze an orange juice container of water in the deep freeze for a couple of days so it is as cold as you can get it. This sort of maxi-cube will last longer than a bunch of small ones.

The gin has to be frozen, too. Always keep gin in the freezer. Boodles is best, Tanquerey is pretty good, but frankly I think a good tonic water is more important than a quality gin. I like Schweppes tonic water and it should be thoroughly chilled, too.

I prefer by far and away to use a slice of real lime—a generous slice—than concentrated, bottled, or whatevered lime. The lime slice should be thrown into the drink so you can contemplate its subtle greens in the clearness of the gin-and-tonic—it's as close as most of us will get to swimming off the CALYPSO.

A gin-and-tonic for cooking should be served in a container large enough that it can not be easily misplaced—at least a pint, preferably a quart and it should be clear glass. NEVER drink a gin-and-tonic through a straw. The ice cube and lime slice should bang up against your nose; it's part of the gin-and-tonic experience.

Make sure that you tell a friend or spouse to check now and then to see if you are burning supper.

See, Bill? Cooking isn't so tough!

109

George Abel ready to grill lamb (not Senator Howard...)

Bus Whitehead and HIS "Whopper."

Rex Amack and one of his views.

110

GOOD SPORTS

Recently Nebraska has been known as the first state in the nation to elect a woman Republican Governor. While that is significant, it should also be noted that Nebraska has produced a leading number of great athletes...as well as offering a first-class list of good sports to participate in. Then, there's the fact that the temperament of the people here generally qualifies most of them as "good sports" of another sort. Here are some stand-outs.

PLATTE RIVER'S PHILLY SANDWICHES

In case you're having a crowd...

Rex Amack, Director,
Game and Parks Commission
Lincoln, NE

---

100 steak buns
200 slices of Swiss American cheese
50-60 green peppers, sliced
40-50 onions, sliced
2 cans (4 lb. 4 oz.) sliced mushrooms, drained
25 lbs. seasoned beef, sliced, at room temperature

Fry onions and peppers on grill until they start to get tender, then add mushrooms and brown lightly. Butter steak buns and brown on grill. Layer beef, grilled vegetables and cheese in bun. Cut sandwiches in half and watch them disappear. Serves 100.

PLATTE RIVER BUFFALO STEW

Rex Amack, Director,
Game and Parks Commission
Lincoln, NE

40 lbs. buffalo tips—cook and drain.
12 1-gal. cans stew vegetables
6 46-oz. cans tomato juice
2 3-lb. 2 oz. cans beef consomme
12 cups cornstarch
6 tbsp. Italian seasoning
6 tbsp. sweet basil leaves
⅓ cup salt
¼ cup pepper
1 cup Worcestershire sauce
½-1 tbsp. liquid smoke
Kitchen Bouquet to desired color

Pour juice from vegetables into stewpot. Add all seasonings, tomato juice and consomme and bring to boil. Thicken with cornstarch. Add vegetables and meat. Cook until heated. Serves 100.

❧

WDO: Game and Parks has some of the very best chefs in Nebraska among its ranks—Rex is one of them. He is doing an admirable job of heading the Nebraska Game and Parks Commission, following the famous footsteps of Gene Mahoney.

PTAKY

My mother gave me this recipe for "Birds In A Blanket" or "Ptaky"—the Czech name—many years ago. It's delicious.
                                        Henry Cech, D.D.S.
                                        Lincoln, NE

Round steak sliced very thin and cut into small pieces, approximately 3″ x 4″–approximately 20 birds per steak.

Chop enough onion and bacon into small pieces to put a small amount in the center of each piece of steak.

Saute onion in 2 tbsp. butter.

Salt and pepper each piece of meat, put onion and bacon in center, roll steak and hold with toothpicks or tie with string.

Put birds in same pan used to saute onion, sprinkle lightly with red pepper and heavily with paprika.

Cook over medium flame for 10 minutes, turning to brown...cover and cook over low flame 2-2½ hours.

To make gravy, remove birds, crush ½ clove garlic into pan juice, use flour and water shaken in a jar to thicken, place birds back into gravy and simmer until warm.

Serve.

❧

WDO: Henry is an orthodontist (whatever that means). He is also a descendant of the old country Czechoslovakia. The "birds" referred to in the recipe are not birds at all. Henry was amazed that I could not follow his Czech "logic" and needed to double "check" to see what he meant by way of birds (blackbirds, quail, hummingbirds, etc.)? It turns out "Czech logic" is somewhat akin to the conflict of terms such as "experienced virgin".

CHOCOLATE REFRIGERATOR CAKE

This is Bob Devaney's favorite dessert. I don't usually unmold it. Instead I use a 9 x 13 cake pan and double the recipe, using vanilla wafer crumbs for top and bottom. Then I chill it well, cut into squares and top with whipped cream to garnish.

Mrs. Bob (Phyllis) Devaney, Wife of Athletic Director
University of Nebraska-Lincoln

Melt 7 oz. package of semi-sweet chocolate chips in a double boiler. Beat in 1 ½ tbsp. water. Remove from heat and add 4 unbeaten egg yolks, one at a time, beating well until smooth.

Beat 4 egg whites stiff, then fold into chocolate mixture. Fold in 1 cup whipped cream. Line the bottom of a casserole or mold with lady fingers or vanilla wafer crumbs and put the chocolate mixture over the lady fingers. Top with more lady fingers. Chill 12 hours. Unmold and garnish with 1 cup of cream, whipped. Nuts may be added to the chocolate mixture if desired.

WDO: Fueled by such delicious desserts as this one, no wonder Bob was able to establish and maintain the winning Big Red tradition.

HOT SMOKED FISH

This recipe was developed in Northern Minnesota after some trial and error. It has been well-received by all, especially after trying several bottles of beer.
Fred Eiche, Member, Lincoln Airport Authority
Lincoln, NE

The greatest problem is catching the fish to smoke. If you do not have access to a lake for the fish, a fish store will do almost as well, though will perhaps not be as much fun.

I like Northern Pike the best — but almost any fish will do.

You need a smoker of the type that the charcoal sits in a bottom pan with a pan of water over that and the grill above the water.

For a fish of 3 to 6 pounds, you will need 7 to 10 pounds of charcoal and a number of large chunks of good hardwood to place on top of the charcoal AFTER they have been soaked in water for at least an hour and the charcoal is well "lit".

The temperature inside the smoker should be a minimum of 120° for 2 hours, then 80-100° for the remainder of smoking time.

Cut the head and tail off the fish which has been gutted. No need to skin or scale.

Soak the fish in solution of 1 cup of coarse salt to 1 gallon of water for 1 hour. Drain and soak again in solution of 4 cups of salt and 2 cups of brown sugar to 1 gallon of water for 2-3 hours.

Remove the fish from the brine and allow to dry for approximately 3 hours. Then place fish in the smoker for anywhere from 8 to 10 hours. When finished, consume with your favorite libation. It will keep, refrigerated, for 2-3 weeks. NEVER freeze smoked fish. It doesn't work.

WDO: Fred deserves special thanks for loaning me his wife, Pam, who helped me put this cookbook together. While I know he likes to cook as well as I do, he may have spent more time in the kitchen because of this book than she did.

SWEET AND SOUR PHEASANT

An unusual treatment for an unusual treat.
Gene Mahoney, Retired Director
Game and Parks Commission
Omaha, NE

1½ lbs. pheasant cut into ½ x 1 inch cubes

Batter:
½ cup flour
¼ cup cornstarch
½ tsp. baking powder
1 tbsp. beaten egg
½ cup water
1 tsp. oil

Dip cubes in batter and deep fat fry in 375° oil until done. Hold in oven until all are cooked.

Sauce:
¾ cup sugar
⅓ cup catsup
1 tbsp. soy sauce
¼ tsp. salt
⅔ cup water
⅓ cup vinegar
Heat until sugar dissolves and thicken with:
3½ tbsp. cornstarch
⅓ cup water
½ tbsp. oil

Add one green pepper cut in bite-size pieces and ½ cup or more pineapple chunks. Heat through and serve over pheasant.

❦

WDO: As former State Senator and Director of the Nebraska Game and Parks Commission, Gene Mahoney endeared himself to the citizens of our state, his employees, and visitors from around the world. He is a unique treasure of which we are very proud.

GRILLED SALMON STEAKS

An unusual ingredient makes these nutritious fish even better for you...and tastier, too.

Tom Osborne, Head Football Coach
University of Nebraska

3 salmon steaks or fillets
1 tsp. miso*
1 tsp. garlic powder
1 tsp. onion powder
1 green pepper, chopped fine

1 tomato, chopped fine
¼ cup onion, chopped fine
1 tsp. pepper

Rinse salmon. Dilute miso with ¼ cup water (or less) to make a pasty texture. Spread miso mixture over fish with pastry brush. Season. Place fish on grill. Top with chopped vegetables. Cover grill and bake until flakey. Do not turn.

* Miso is a soybean paste most easily found in Oriental food stores. It should be stored in the refrigerator.

TOM'S OATMEAL COOKIES

1 cup flour
½ tsp. baking soda
¼ tsp. cinnamon
1½ cups quick oats
1 cup raisins softened
2 egg whites, beaten

1 cup brown sugar
⅓ cup safflower oil
½ cup skim milk
1 tsp. vanilla
nuts, shredded carrots, dates*

* optional

One 6 oz. can frozen concentrated apple juice, undiluted, can be substituted for the brown sugar. Mix all ingredients and drop on greased cookie sheet. Bake 12 minutes at 350°.

❦

WDO: Tom's reputation as a fisherman is legend. His favorite spots are a well-guarded secret (I don't blame him). In his spare time, he coaches Nebraska football in a fashion that is the envy of just about anyone who knows anything about the game. He is also a gentleman of the "first order" and a wonderful role model for the young men who are privileged to play on his teams.

HUNTER/FISHERMAN OUTDOOR RECIPE

This will literally keep for days uncooked in a cooler.
Chuck Sand, Owner, Sand Livestock Systems
Columbus, NE

1) take triple layer of heavy aluminum foil 24″ square
2) dice beef, pork or wild meat in about 1″ lean cubes
3) slice cubes of potatoes, onions, tomatoes and peppers
4) salt sparingly, pepper liberally
5) add ice cubes (for moisture)
6) wrap and seal foil well

Can be cooked on the coals of an outdoor campfire for 20-30 minutes for a super outdoor pre-prepared meal.

WDO: Chuck and Carol Sand are the epitome of the entrepreneurs in Nebraska. They own several businesses which have succeeded not only in our state, but in the Far East. They know more about Hong Kong and mainland China than most people in the Diplomatic Corps.

BANNOCK

This hot bread will make you a hero in a hunting camp...
James Stuart, Sr., Stuart Investment Company
Lincoln, NE

1 cup flour
1½ tsp. baking powder
2 tbsp. bacon fat
cold water

Knead together (as bread) and flatten or roll with a round whiskey bottle to fit bottom of fry pan...

Brown on bottom over campfire...then tip up pan by fire and brown and "bake" until just right...

WDO: Jim Stuart is one of the leaders of the Lincoln banking/financial industry. Someone said that Jim reminds them of James Cagney. That is a compliment to both men.

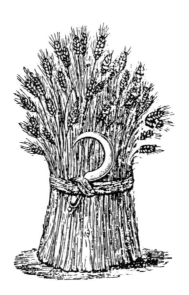

PHEASANT SUPREME

Since this recipe was originally given to me by my sister-in-law from Iowa (a good Republican by the way), it only works well with Iowa pheasant! Wild ones! Shot squarely behind the eye with ONE (and only one) BB. Therefore requires a hunter of excellent marksmanship! (Try a Democrat...hear they're good at pot-shot taking.)

CeAnn Zanotti
Omaha, NE

---

6 pheasant breasts, boned and cubed
orange juice to cover pheasant
1 clove garlic, minced
¼-½ cup raisins with sherry to cover
½ cup sherry
½ cup slivered almonds
½ cup sliced green olives
4 oz. olive oil
1½ sticks butter or margarine
flour
1 sm. bunch parsley, cut up with kitchen shears

Marinate cubes of pheasant in orange juice, garlic and parsley for 3 hours refrigerated. Marinate raisins in sherry for 1 hour.

After marinating, remove pheasant from liquid and dust with flour. Brown in olive oil. Drain oil. In small saucepan, melt butter, add sherry, heat to a glaze. Add almonds, olives and raisins. Pour mixture over pheasant pieces; simmer covered for 45 minutes to 1 hour. Serve over wild rice or rice of choice.

NEBRASKA NOTABLES WESTERN AND OTHERWISE

Other states may have had more notables, but no state has more notables for its size than Nebraska. You may challenge this statement, but will be called on to prove it to me. (Another sticky issue, peanut-butterwise?) In all seriousness, Kay and I are proud of Nebraska's people.

MACAROON DESSERT

Tom Dorwart, County Judge
Sidney, NE

2 dozen almond macaroons
1 large can condensed milk
milk
½ cup cornstarch (less than)
½ cup sugar
1 tsp. vanilla extract
2 egg whites, beaten

Pour condensed milk into quart container. Add enough milk to make a quart. Pour into double boiler and stir in less than ½ cup cornstarch while cooking. Keep stirring and add ½ cup sugar.

Stir about 20 minutes or until well-thickened. Remove from heat. Add 1 tsp. vanilla. Have egg whites well-beaten and fold in. Put layer of macaroons in bowl, cover with liquid and keep alternating cookies and liquid. Chill well and serve with a dollop of currant jelly or strawberry jam. Top with whipped cream. (I prefer Wolferman's Jelly and Empress Jam.)

WDO: Sidney, Nebraska is more than 400 miles west of Lincoln. A distinguished judge, Tom and his wife, Pat, are among the great citizens of that city. It always amazes me that they are faithful in attending both political and non-political meetings held in Lincoln, as are many other Western Nebraskans. These people are a driving force in our state in every sense of the word!

SANDHILL
STEAK STRIPS

This one may be cooked in a skillet or a wok, depending on your utensil inventory and/or preferences.

Tedd Huston, Attorney
Broken Bow, NE

---

4 cups hot cooked rice
1 lb. lean beef round steak, thinly
sliced into 1 inch strips
3 tbsp. vegetable oil
2 cups each sliced onions and carrots
⅓ cup burgundy wine
2 cups beef broth
4 oz. can sliced mushrooms
2 ½ tsp. seasoned salt
1 tbsp. Worcestershire sauce
2 cups sliced celery
2 tbsp. cornstarch

While rice cooks, saute steak in oil until brown. Add onions and cook 2 minutes longer. Stir in carrots, wine, broth, mushrooms and seasonings. Bring to boil, reduce heat, cover and simmer for 10 minutes. Add celery and continue cooking 10 minutes longer. Dissolve cornstarch in ¼ cup water. Stir into meat mixture. Cook, stirring occasionally until thickened. Serve over rice. Serves 6.

❦

WDO: When Tedd isn't cooking, he practices law. He is also a great conversationalist and it is a pleasure to visit with him about Broken Bow, the "greater Nebraska" area, or anything else for that matter.

GOOSEBERRY SALAD

Wayne L. Johnson
Ainsworth, NE

#2 can gooseberries
1 cup sugar
3 oz. package of lime Jello
3 oz. package of lemon Jello
½ cup pecans (optional)
1 cup celery, diced
½ cup grated Velveeta cheese
dash of salt

Drain liquid from berries and add enough water to it to make 2 cups liquid. Add the sugar and heat to boiling. Pour over the 2 Jellos and mix until dissolved. Add 1¾ cups cold water, berries, celery, cheese and pecans. Chill, stirring occasionally.

WDO: These both sounded interesting, so both were included!

SAUCY CRANBERRY DESSERT

Rich, but delicious.

Wayne L. Johnson
Ainsworth, NE

2 cups flour
1 cup sugar
3 tsp. baking powder
½ tsp. salt
1 cup milk
3 tbsp. soft oleo or butter
1 tsp. vanilla

Combine above, beat 3 minutes at medium speed.

Add 2 cups raw cranberries whole. Bake in greased 9″ square or 11x7″ pan at 350° for 25-30 minutes.

Note: a single batch of the Velvet Crumb Cake recipe on the Bisquick box can be substituted for the cake portion above.

Butter Sauce:
1 cup sugar
¾ cup light cream
½ cup butter (do not use oleo)

Combine these three ingredients and heat to boiling. Serve hot over the dessert squares. Serves 10-12.

FRUIT AND NUT COOKIES

This cookie recipe puts all others in the background as far as I'm concerned. My wife, Elaine, created it.
        Bob Moreland, Owner, Green Valley Hereford Ranch
                                                    Merriman, NE

1 cup shortening
1 cup brown sugar
1 cup white sugar
2 eggs
1 tsp. vanilla
2 cups flour
1 tsp. soda
pinch of salt
1 cup raisins
½ cup chopped dates
½ cup chopped nuts

Beat first five ingredients together. Sift together next three ingredients and add to first mixture. Mix in last three ingredients and drop by teaspoon onto greased cookie sheet. Bake at 350⁰ until done. Makes about 5 dozen cookies.

WDO: One of Nebraska's most outstanding Sandhills spreads is the Moreland's Green Valley Hereford Ranch. I'm still grateful for the iced tea given to Kay and me one day after we had just traveled there from the Bowring ranch, some 20 miles away, in 90⁰+ temperatures. In return, Bob got to lobby the Governor.

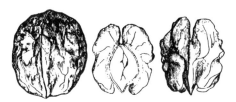

COME 'N GET IT SOUR CREAM RAISIN PIE

This gets everybody to the table every time I make it.
Mimi Lou Moody, Rancher's Wife
Crawford, NE

Mix:
1½ cup sugar
½ tsp. nutmeg
1 tsp. cinnamon
1 tsp. allspice
2 tbsp. flour

Mix:
2 tsp. melted butter
4 egg yolks
3 tbsp. vinegar
1½ cups sour cream

Gradually add 1½ cups softened raisins. Combine all and cook slowly till just boiling. Cool. Pour into baked pie shell.

Use 4 egg whites for meringue; bake at 350° for 15-20 minutes.

Ed Note: Mimi Lou has one of the best "samplers" hanging in her kitchen I've ever seen. It says, "A good hostess is a lot like a duck; calm on the surface and paddling like hell underneath".

NEBRASKA SNAKE RIVER TROUT

A delicacy that can be fixed both plain (but delicious) and fancy (also delicious-see page 82).

Bill Mulligan, The Bootery
Valentine, NE

---

requisite number of fish for people
2-3 strips of bacon per fish
garlic salt
fresh ground pepper
real butter
aluminum foil

Remove head and thoroughly wash each cleaned fish. Preheat oven to 350°. Cut foil to wrap each fish completely. Season fish with garlic salt and fresh ground pepper on one side (not the inner cavity). Lay that side on top of the first strip of bacon. Spread butter on top side of fish, season again with garlic salt and fresh ground pepper. Cover with second strip of bacon or wrap strips around if preferred. Wrap in foil and seal completely. Bake for 30 minutes or to preference.

Release trout (delicate and very moist) for immediate enjoyment!

WDO: Kay and I took a trip down the Snake River (Surprise! Nebraska has one, too.) It is all on private grounds and deserves its name. Much like a snake. Try it—you MAY like it.

FILET
TETE-A-TETE FLAMBE

An elegant party entree!

Robert Allen, Board of Regents
University of Nebraska, Hastings, NE

1 whole beef tenderloin
4 tbsp. butter
¼ cup green onion, chopped
3 tsp. prepared mustard
2 tsp. soy sauce
¾ cup sherry
1/8 tsp. pepper
¼ cup cognac (warmed slightly)
parsley to garnish

Place tenderloin in baking dish and spread generously with butter. Bake in oven at 400° for about 35 minutes. Then pour over the tenderloin a sauce made by combining all other ingredients except cognac. (Cook sauce first until it has reduced by about ⅓.) Put meat in oven again and bake about 10 minutes longer. Place on warm platter and spoon juices over. Garnish with parsley. Pour warmed cognac over meat — flame and serve.

POPPY'S FLUFFY POPOVERS

Keep grandchildren out of kitchen while baking these or your favorite fluffy popovers will look like flapjacks! (They're good this way, too. Serve with maple syrup.)
Steve Carveth, M.D., Cardio-Vascular Surgeon
Lincoln, NE

Contents:
1 cup flour
¼ tsp. salt (omit for heart patients; use salt substitute)
1 tsp. sugar (omit for diabetics)
1 tbsp. melted butter (heart patients, use vegetable oil)
1 cup milk
2 eggs

Description of operation:

Stir together flour, salt and sugar with much vigor in your favorite mixing bowl until contents are blended. Add butter, milk and eggs. Beat until smooth as silk (about 2.36 minutes). While beating, scape bowl frequently with rubber spatula to keep your favorite bowl relatively clean. With Crisco, grease containers (metal muffin pans or oven proof glass custard cups) and pour—very carefully—previously made contents into your choice of container(s). Fill each container .5 full. For a rich, golden brown shell with damp interior, bake on center rack at 400 º for 41 minutes or until well browned and firm to your tender touch. For a lighter, pale brown popover with dry interior, bake at 375 º for 56 minutes. Keep oven door closed at all times. Remove your fluffy popovers from containers and serve hot. Makes 8-12 super fluffy popovers.

❧

WDO: A cardiovascular surgeon of national repute, Steve says his office hours are 12-6 (between fluffy popovers). Steve was instrumental in establishing the Red Cross First Aid volunteers at UNL home football games, a program that has been emulated at many other schools across the country. In addition to his precise medical—and popover—expertise, Steve has an intense interest in good government and good conversation.

VEGETABLE BEEF SOUP

This was a favorite when Dick was at home...and still is!
Dorcas Cavett
Lincoln, NE

Simmer 2-3 beef shank bones in 1 qt. water in crock pot or on stove for several hours until the meat falls off the bones. Remove bones. Then add these vegetables all cleaned and diced into small pieces:

3-4 potatoes
1-2 medium onions
3 carrots
½ head of cabbage.

Add 1 can stewed tomatoes, 1 small can tomato sauce, 1 can string beans. Add very little salt. (I never use peas or corn in this soup.) Simmer all ingredients until tender and tasty. Serve piping hot!

❧

WDO: I can smell this cooking just by reading the recipe!

GALLIANO CHICKEN WINGS

Ed. Note: What's better than living next door to two great cooks who like to share their concoctions? Nothing.
Jerry and Tish Druliner
Eaton, Tinstman, Druliner, Inc.
Lincoln, NE

---

2 dozen chicken wings
(have butcher chop off the tip ends)

Place chicken in shallow non-metal dish. Cover with following marinade:

---

1 tbsp. dried tarragon
2 tsp. grated lemon peel
⅓ cup lemon juice
½ cup Galliano liqueur

Marinate in refrigerator for several hours or overnight. Turn pieces occasionally.

Cook by pan frying or oven frying (arrange in a single layer, drizzle with butter and bake at 400° 10 minutes or until brown. Turn and baste with drippings, then bake 10 minutes longer.)

❧

WDO: I'm told these are as good left over as they are in the first place. Trouble is, I don't think there'll ever BE any left over when I make them.

LEMON ZEST CHICKEN

This is a very versatile recipe for chicken. It can be baked in the oven and served with a sauce or it can be grilled. It is low in cholesterol, saturated fats and salt, but does not lack in flavor. The secret is the lemon zest.

John R. Fischer, M.D., Prairie Medical Center
Omaha, NE

6 single chicken breasts, boned and skinned
1 tsp. Dash seasoning (optional)
2 tsp. corn starch
Marinade:
¼ cup Italian salad dressing
juice from one lemon
2 tsp. finely diced red bell pepper
zest from two lemons (peel lemon skins off with potato peeler and chop very, very fine)
1 tsp. Dash seasoning
(and/or season with small amounts of salt and pepper)
¼ cup of chicken broth or boullion

Slightly flatten the chicken breasts with a mallet and place in the marinade for at least two hours. Remove breasts and dust with cornstarch and Dash. If you wish to grill the chicken at this point, baste with the marinade and make sure you place the marinade sediment on top of the chicken as it is cooking. When the chicken feels spongy it is done. Do not overcook.

To cook in the oven, place in a single layer in a pan so that they tightly fit; pour in the marinade and make sure to put the marinade sediment on top of the chicken. Cook at 375° for about 20-25 minutes. Do not overcook as the chicken will dry out. Put the pan juices over the chicken before serving.

Serve this dish with boiled new potatoes or rice. A good California Chardonnay is a perfect match.

GREAT CHOCOLATE AND BROWNIES, TOO

The secret ingredient in this chocolate lover's brownie is the cold coffee in the frosting!
William A. Fitzgerald, President/CEO,
Commercial Federal
Omaha, NE

---

2 cups sugar
melt and cool:
4 oz. unsweetened chocolate squares
½ pound butter
beat 4 eggs, add ¼ tsp. salt

Add sugar gradually; fold in melted mixture; add 1 cup flour and 1 cup chopped nuts (optional); bake at 325° for 25-30 minutes; (use 9x13 or jelly roll pan – greased).

FROSTING:
Melt 1 stick butter or oleo
Add 6 tbsp. cocoa
6 tbsp. cold coffee
1 pound box powdered sugar
2 tsp. vanilla

WDO: And he said he doesn't cook!

BUTTER TOFFEE BARS

Only a few ingredients, but a LOT of good flavor...
Natalie Hahn
Polk, NE

1 cup oleo
1 cup brown sugar
1 egg
2 cups flour
1 tsp. vanilla

Mix above ingredients together and pat into 9 x 12 pan.
Bake at 350⁰ for 15 to 20 minutes.

Remove from oven and top with 1 cup of chocolate chips.
Spread over top of mix as they melt. Cool and cut into bars.

CHICKEN BREAST MARSALA

This is a dinner of select slices of chicken breast meat in an elegant Marsala wine sauce served with noodles Nicoise. Green beans in butter sauce complement this renowned Italian recipe.
Mike Harper, Chairman/CEO, ConAgra
Omaha, NE

To prepare in microwave:

...remove ARMOUR CLASSIC FROZEN DINNER by the same name from carton;

...cut a small slit in center of film cover;

...heat on HIGH 5 to 7 minutes or until hot, rotating plate once;

...let stand 2 to 3 minutes before serving;

...remove lid carefully.

This will be one of the finest recipes to appear in your cookbook – it's certainly going to be one of the easiest to prepare! Only 270 calories and can be purchased for under $3.00.

❦

WDO: Mike goes about cooking in much the same way he goes about almost everything. He gets on with it. Also note his tendency to get maximum dollar value, low caloric count and a big bang for the buck. (Guess who owns Armour Foods?)

139

JOHN'S BBQ RIBS

A happy marriage with the Cheezy Potatoes—and I'm not kidding.

John S. Katelman, Attorney
Omaha, NE

Start with nice, meaty pork back ribs (spare ribs will do if you can't find back ribs). Season with your favorite salt, pepper and spice concoctions. (I use Lawry's Seasoned Salt & Seasoned Pepper, garlic powder and celery salt.) Then add the crucial ingredient—celery seed. Sprinkle it liberally on both sides of the ribs. Then cook them slowly on the grill. Another secret—take your time. If you have guests, make sure they are hungry. (It's remarkable what a couple of hours and a few drinks will do for their appetites and appreciation of your culinary genius.) When the ribs are done, take them off the grill, set them on aluminum foil, pour on plenty of your favorite sauce, wrap them up and put them back on the grill for a couple of minutes until you can hear the sauce bubbling. Then serve. (Don't cook them with the sauce on them—it's too much work and too hard to keep them from burning.)

❦

WDO: These two people fell in love with each other and decided to combine recipes. She says the potato recipe was part of the first meal she ever prepared for him and "could've had something to do with it". Who am I to argue?

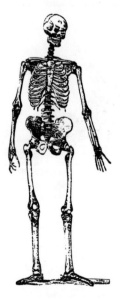

CHEEZY POTATOES

This is a great dish to take to dinner parties and goes great with about anything. Men just go wild over it, so you never have to worry about leftovers.
Lynn Bauer Katelman, Real Estate Broker
Omaha, NE

---

3 packages thawed hashbrown patties (4 to a package)
1 can cream of chicken soup
1 carton sour cream (¾ of big size)
Lawry's seasoned salt and pepper to your liking
1 bunch green onions, cut up

Place hashbrowns in greased 9 x 13 dish. Mix other ingredients and pour over potatoes. Grate American cheese to cover top and crush 1 small bag potato chips to cover cheese. Melt ½ stick butter and pour over top. Bake at 350° covered with foil for 30 minutes. Remove foil and cook for additional half hour at same temperature.

ELEGANT, EASY BEEF TENDERLOIN

This is our family "panic" recipe for impromptu dinner party
fare. It only takes 10 minutes to prepare!
Bruce Lauritzen, President/CEO, First National Bank
Omaha, NE

Brush whole beef tenderloin with olive oil.
Bake at 425° for 45 minutes.
Slice with electric knife.
Pour following mixture over sliced tenderloin:

1 stick melted butter
2 cans button mushrooms, drained
garlic salt to taste
1 tbsp. Worcestershire sauce
¼ lb. blue cheese
1 tsp. onion salt
¼ tsp. caraway seeds (optional)

WDO: All of a sudden, Bruce has "become" a great cook...and
an outstanding banker. What more could wife Kim hope for?

APPLE-CHEESE SALAD

An old favorite, except I prefer to leave the nuts out of the cream cheese filling.

Martin Massengale, Chancellor
University of Nebraska-Lincoln

---

1 cup hot water
⅔ cup (6 oz.) small red cinnamon candies
1 package lemon gelatin
1½ cup sweetened applesauce
8 oz. package cream cheese
½ cup chopped nuts (optional)
½ cup fine cut celery
½ cup mayonnaise-type salad dressing

Pour hot water over cinnamon candies. Stir until they dissolve. Add gelatin; stir until it completely dissolves. Add applesauce. Pour half the mixture into an 8 inch square pan*. Let chill until firm.

Blend together cream cheese (at room temperature) nuts and celery. Add salad dressing. Spread in a layer over firm apple mixture. Pour on remaining apple mixture. Chill until firm; unmold; garnish with small bunches of sugared grapes. Makes 6 servings.

* To fill a 5½ cup star mold, you'll need 1½ recipes of apple mixture and 1 recipe of cream cheese filling.

WDO: Martin is also a member of Woodmen's Board of Directors. Good leadership combined with a great sense of humor make this man a welcome citizen of the state.

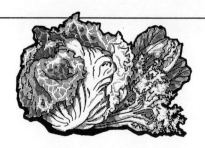

BLENDER COCKTAIL AND VEGETABLE SALAD

Here's an unlikely dish designed for the man who's not sure he can even boil water in the kitchen. If you hop to it, this strange fruit and vegetable combination can be whipped out in less than 10 minutes. The ladies who know all about what's cookin' will probably say, "ridiculous concoction". The youngsters will probably groan, "yuck". However, when served, all will say, "by golly, this is good". So, guys, get out your electric blender, a can of those cubed chunks of fruit cocktail and become an instant chef.

David Meisenholder
Lincoln, NE

---

1 cup carrots, sliced 1 inch thick
1 stalk celery, sliced 1 inch thick
¼ small onion, quartered
¼ small green pepper
½ cup well-drained canned fruit cocktail
½ tsp. seasoned salt
2 tbsp. mayonnaise

Place vegetables in blender, cover with water, put on blender cap. Flick switch to high speed — on for a few seconds — off — then on/off two or three times to chop vegetables.

Drain thoroughly. Press out excess moisture between paper towels. Transfer to bowl and lightly mix in fruit cocktail, salt and mayonnaise.

Serve on bed of crisp lettuce. Serves 4.

❧

WDO: This gentleman is one who appreciates good food, but is more dedicated to playing the piano and accompanying yours truly in song. It is not to Dave's credit that he thinks I am a good singer. Who knows, he may be a "great" chef just as I may be a "great" singer.

CHEDDAR CHEESE AND BRANDY SOUP

You may've had brandy and cheese together before, but I'll bet it wasn't like this...
> William R. Nester, President, Kearney State College
> Kearney, NE

In a soup pot, melt ¼ cup butter; add one finely diced onion and saute until transparent.

Add:
½ cup flour
2 tbsp. chicken base
1 tsp. curry powder
1 tsp. paprika
½ cup finely chopped celery
4 cups milk or light cream or chicken stock
Stir, bring to a boil and add:
1 cup dry sherry
1½ cups extra sharp cheddar cheese, grated
Just before serving, add:
3 tbsp. fresh bacon bits
¼ cup brandy
2-3 tbsp. chopped parsley
4 friends

❦

WDO: This man is responsible for bringing Kearney State College from good to excellent. He admits to being a good cook, but an even greater appreciator of good food cooked by someone else.

BETTER THAN
SEX CAKE

*Not an original with me...taken from a magazine of some
description some time ago.*

William O. Nielsen, Mayor
Franklin, NE

1 package yellow cake mix
(2 layer size, pudding in the mix)
20 oz. can crushed pineapple
1 cup sugar
6 oz. package vanilla pudding mix (regular or instant)
8 oz. container frozen whipped topping, thawed
1 cup flaked coconut (approximatly)
1 cup chopped pecans (approximately)
maraschino cherries (optional)

Prepare cake according to package directions and bake in
a 9x13 pan. Meanwhile combine crushed pineapple
(undrained) with sugar and bring to a boil. Boil five minutes.
Immediately after cake has been removed from oven, pour
syrup over hot cake. Allow to cool completely.

Prepare pudding mix according to package directions. (Some
recipes suggest folding coconut into the pudding). Spread
pudding over the cooled cake. Top with whipped topping
and sprinkle with coconut (if you didn't put it in the pudding) and pecans. If desired, garnish with maraschino
cherries.

Variations: slice three bananas and arrange slices over cake
after adding syrup and cooling; continue as directed with
pudding and toppings. The whipped topping may be
replaced with one cup whipping cream whipped with ¼ cup
confectioners sugar and 1 tsp. vanilla. If desired, toast the
flaked coconut.

❧

*WDO: I'm not touching this one, opinionwise, that is. You be
the judge.*

146

PLATTE VALLEY MUD PIE

Serves 8 persons or 2 husbands if their wives aren't present!
Ed Nielsen, Nielsen Chevrolet, Buick, Mazda
Columbus, NE

---

21 oreo cookies
6 tbsp. melted butter
1 qt. chocolate ice cream
1 tbsp. instant coffee granules
2 tbsp. instant Sanka
½ pt. whipping cream, whipped
2 tbsp. brandy
2 tbsp. kahlua
12 oz. jar of fudge topping

Crush cookies very fine and mix with butter. Press into 9″ pie pan. Freeze. Whip together ice cream, coffees, 4 tbsp. whipped cream, brandy and kahlua. Pour into frozen pie shell. Freeze until very hard. Spread fudge over pie with a knife dipped in hot water. Return to freezer. Serve with remaining whipped cream.

WDO: With apologies to Ed's Chevrolet dealership, I think this recipe ought to be the "heartbeat of America"...who could NOT like it?

147

APPLESAUCE BARS

Moist, marvelous and makes a lot!
Susie Rasmussen, A "Retired" Chef
Omaha, NE

Cream:
1½ cups sugar
½ cup margarine
1 egg
1 tsp. vanilla
Sift together:
2 cups flour
1 tsp. cinnamon
½ tsp. nutmeg
½ tsp. ground cloves
2 tsp. baking soda
½ tsp. salt

Add alternately with 1½ cups applesauce (flour first and last). Add 1 cup raisins (heated in hot water to "plump" up and drained). Add 1 cup chopped nuts.

Mix and put into sheet cake pan. Bake for 25 minutes at 350° in preheated oven.

Icing:
½ cup margarine
1 cup brown sugar
¼ cup milk

Bring to boil and boil hard for 1 minute. Add 1 tsp. vanilla and 1 cup sifted powdered sugar. Beat till spreadable and spread on warm cake. Cut in bars when cool.

❧

WDO: In a state that grows so many great apples, we had to include some great apple recipes. This is one of them. You'll find others on pages 5, 143 and 246.

GERMAN POTATO SALAD

*This "make ahead" potato dish is a favorite and goes well with
any of the German dishes I was raised on.*
Ronald W. Roskens, President, University of Nebraska
Lincoln, NE

8 slices bacon
1 medium onion, diced
2 tbsp. flour
½ cup vinegar
½ cup water
½ cup sugar
4 tsp. salt
pepper to taste
8 cups (4-5 lbs.) potatoes, cooked in skins

Fry bacon until crisp; crumble and reserve. Saute onion in
drippings. Add flour, vinegar, water, sugar, salt and pepper.
Cook until thickened. Add crumbled bacon.

Pour over sliced potatoes. Garnish with parsley. Serve hot.
Can be assembled in baking dish and reheated in oven at
serving time.

HARDTACK

This is a thin, crispy cracker that I discovered in my constant search for a low-calorie, nutritious snack.
Ronald W. Roskens, President,University of Nebraska
Lincoln, NE

1 cup quick oatmeal (raw)
1 cup bran buds
1 cup flour
¼ cup sugar (half that is plenty)
Stir together in a bowl and set aside.

½ stick oleo
½ cup boiling water
½ tsp. soda

Melt oleo in water, then add soda. Stir liquid into dry ingredients to thoroughly moisten. Divide dough into 3 balls.

Grease a flat (no sides) cookie sheet VERY WELL.

Roll dough, a third at a time, on cookie sheet as thinly as possible, lightly flouring rolling pin if needed.

Sprinkle flattened dough lightly with salt. Prick with fork every inch or so. Score in 1 to ½ inch squares with pizza cutter or knife. Bake in 350° oven for 12-15 minutes. Remove from pan while hot. Store in cool, dry place in tightly covered container.

WDO: Ron and I knew each other at the University of Iowa back in the 50's. (That was when he had hair.) He has not spent a lot of time trying to grow hair. Rather, his commitment has been to excellence in education and toward this end he continues to strive today. Ron married another Iowan—Lois—she is dynamite and helps Ron all the way.

LASAGNE

Wow! I coulda made it with V-8. (Now you can...and you don't have to cook the noodles, either.)

Mike Schilling
Pawnee City, NE

1 lb. lean ground beef
1 cup chopped onion
3 cloves garlic, crushed

Brown above ingredients and drain fat.
Add:

4 cups V-8 vegetable juice
8 oz. fresh mushrooms
6 oz. can tomato paste
1 tbsp. Worcestershire sauce
1 tsp. oregano
1 tsp. basil
1 tsp. parsley
½ tsp. salt
1/8 tsp. pepper

Simmer with hamburger mixture for 30 minutes.

1 package lasagne noodles, uncooked
15-oz. package cottage or ricotta cheese
1-1½ cups Parmesan cheese
2 cups shredded mozarella cheese

In 9 x 13 pan layer ½ of noodles, sauce and cheeses. Repeat and top with parsley if desired. Cover with foil and bake for 30 minutes at 350°. Remove foil; bake 15 minutes longer. Let stand for 20 minutes before cutting.

❧

WDO: Mike married one of our daughter's best friends and is now the father of two beautiful children. This lasagne is evidence you may be able to keep 'em down on the farm, but they can still cook Italian!

FILLET OF SOLE IN WHITE WINE SAUCE

This is an elegant, simple recipe given to me by a friend from Connecticut.

Mrs. Ed (Margie) Scribante, Wife of Founder
Majers, Corp.
Omaha, NE

---

6 fillets of sole
muenster cheese (enough for 12 1/8″ thick slices)
white cooking wine (dry)
butter or margarine

Cut fillets in half lengthwise — place a slice of cheese on each half. Roll up and secure with a toothpick. Place in baking dish, put a daub of butter on each and drizzle with white wine. Bake at 350° for 30 minutes or until fish is white and flakes. Serves 6-8.

❧

WDO: Ed is the founding father of Majers Corp., one of the most successful businesses in Nebraska, which he unashamedly sold for "a fortune". Sounds good to me. He is also blessed with a great family of promising children. A hard combination to beat.

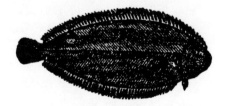

AMBER CREAM

Taken from a Gold Medal Flour Cookbook dated 1914. Sent to us by Bill Duffy who notes that Mrs. A.C. Shallenberger, who submitted the original recipe, was the wife of a former Nebraska Governor.

1 qt. milk
½ package gelatin
1 cup sugar
yolks of 6 eggs
whites of 6 eggs
1 tsp. vanilla

Dissolve gelatin in a little cold water. Let milk come to boiling point and melt gelatin in it. Add sugar and well-beaten yolks of eggs, stirring constantly until well blended. Cook in a double boiler until thickened, then fold in whites of eggs whipped to a stiff froth. Flavor with vanilla. Pour into cups or a fancy mold and set in a cold place overnight. When ready to serve, turn out on a plate or sauce dish.

❧

WDO: Our thanks for this bit of history, which adds a certain degree of nostalgic charm to the book. I like that! I even looked up her picture in the gallery of First Ladies (which is now a gallery of First Ladies and...me).

ELEGANT CHEESECAKE

Instead of the typical sour cream, this recipe uses lemon juice and sweet cream...a little different, and maybe lighter taste.
Steve Siel, LEAD V
Franklin, NE

14 2x2" graham cracker squares
2 tbsp. sugar
¼ cup margarine
juice of 1 lemon
3 8-oz. packages cream cheese, softened
1 cup sugar
2 tbsp. flour
3 eggs
¼ cup light cream
buttered springform pan

Roll graham crackers into fine crumbs and then add 2 tbsp. sugar and melted margarine. Press onto bottom and half-way up the sides of a prepared pan. Place cream cheese in mixing bowl. Squeeze lemon juice over cheese. Mix together until smooth, then add sugar and flour. Add eggs and blend until smooth. Add cream, thoroughly blend. Pour mixture into prepared baking pan. Bake 15 minutes at 450°. Reduce oven to 200° and bake 1 hour. Turn off oven and allow cheesecake to remain in oven 10 minutes. Remove and cool thoroughly. Remove sides of springform pan. Add 1 can cherry pie filling on top.

ITALIAN SHEET CAKE

Coconut lovers will find this recipe especially appealing...
Perry L. Slocum, Chairman of the Board
Franklin (NE) State Bank

Cream together:
1½ cups sugar
1 stick oleo
½ cup shortening
Add 5 egg yolks.
Add alternately:
2 cups flour
1 tsp. soda
1 cup buttermilk
Add:
1 tsp. vanilla
1½ cups coconut
1 cup chopped nuts

Fold in 5 stiffly beaten egg whites.
Bake in greased sheet pan at 350° for 25-30 minutes.

Frost with:
8 oz. cream cheese
½ stick oleo
1 lb. powdered sugar
1 tsp. vanilla
more coconut or nuts if desired

(This makes a lot of frosting.)

FUDGE

When preparing this, I've been told that the only ingredient I can find is the kitchen itself.
Willis Strauss, Retired Chairman, Enron
Omaha, NE

---

2 cups sugar
⅔ cup milk (cream is better)
2 squares Bakers chocolate
1 large piece butter (almost ¼ lb.)

Put all in a pan and cook, stirring constantly, until a firm ball is formed in a cup of cold water. Place pan in cold water. Add vanilla and nuts. Beat until almost set. Pour into greased pan.

❧

WDO: Inasmuch as Bill has been right more often than he has been wrong, both of his recipes have been included. Sort of a sweet 'n sauer combination, you might say. (See page 262 for explanation.)

BBQ RIBS

Time itself is the ingredient, the short commodity, that makes this recipe work for you. Hot, satisfying and easy means you can execute this plan and put a first-class meal on the plate with minimal time spent—about 5 minutes or less!
Scott Stuart, President Imperial Outdoor Advertising
Lincoln, NE

---

1) Country style ribs—with bones or boneless. I prefer with bones. Figure 2-3 ribs per person, plus 2-3 for leftovers. These are even better, if possible, the second day.

2) Bottle BBQ Sauce—I prefer Heinz original recipe; save ¼ cup for dipping later. Yum!

3) ⅓-½ cup orange juice—fresh.

4) 1 orange sliced ¼" thick and spread around the ribs. If the rind is thick, remove 50% of it or it makes the ribs too bitter.

Place all this in your crockpot and set on low heat for 8 to 10 hours. Serve with applesauce and cole slaw. Spend about two hours dreaming up a story about how hard you worked to make something this good!

WDO: Scott is a friend, a pilot and an outstanding cook. Not necessarily in that order, but not necessarily not in that order, either. (Maybe I should say ORRder...?)

LEGENDARY TEXAS CHILI

Prior to concocting—or consuming—this chili, you might be interested in "The Legend of the Longhorn". It goes as follows:

This is the chili famous for the fact that—according to legend (Texas legend, that is)—it was a staple in the diet of those hardy cowboys who drove cattle from the Highlands of the Big Bend Country in Texas to the nearest railroad at Abilene, Kansas. A little-known fact is that—according to legend (Texas legend, that is)—these original cattle were actually shorthorns. The legend has it that these shorthorns—always inquisitive critters—located a pot of left-over chili one cool autumn night and devoured it—all of it. Stimulated by the extraordinarily warm spirit and spice of the chili, these SHORThorns became LONGhorns! And that is how the famous Texas Longhorns came to be.

Postscript: The muscular nature of this chili has been weakened by successive generations of tenderfeet...hence you may consume great quantities with minimal physical distortions and only slight gastronomical discomfort. So says Texas legend...
D.B. "Woody" Varner, Chairman Emeritas
University of Nebraska Foundation
Lincoln, NE

Brown 2 lbs. of ground hamburger
in small amount of bacon fat

Add:

2 tbsp. chili powder
6 oz. can of tomato paste
2 cloves garlic put through garlic press
water to desired consistency
2 tsp. salt and ¼ tsp. black pepper
1 tsp. cumin seed

Simmer all day, adding water when necessary.

Sometimes true Yankees will want to add beans. If you qualify, go ahead; it's your chili. On the other hand, true Texans may want to step up the infusion of chili powder and/or red pepper. Feel free to do so at your own risk, but first—reread the legend of the longhorn above.

TEXAS TACOS

Another delectable dish from down 'dat direction...
Woody Varner

Chop 1 lg. onion
2 ½ lbs. ground chuck
2 cloves of garlic put through garlic press
2 ½ tsp. salt
¼ tsp. black pepper
2 med. fresh tomatoes, peeled and chopped
1 tbsp. chili powder
½ tsp. cumin
½ tsp. coriander
1 tsp. oregano

Cook onion, garlic and meat until brown and meat is well broken up. Add remaining ingredients and simmer for 12-15 minutes.

Place 2-3 tbsp. of above meat mixture into each heated taco shell; fill shells with chopped tomatoes, chopped lettuce and grated cheese. For added spirit, pour on Pace Picante Sauce to taste.

🌳

WDO: Woody and Paula have had a profound influence upon the University of Nebraska and the entire state. How fortunate that Texas let him "go north"! We don't mind the southern influence, as long as Varners keep calling Nebraska "home". When Kay was elected Governor, I gave one piece of advice: never follow Woody Varner as a speaker! Some people may have to; no one can.

FRENCH BREAD

A classic you really CAN make yourself...go ahead and try it.
Del Weber, Chancellor
University of Nebraska-Omaha

1 tbsp. salt
1 tbsp. salad oil
1 tbsp. sugar
1 envelope dry yeast
5-5½ cups flour
egg whites

Mix salt, salad oil and sugar in 1 cup of boiling water. Add one cup of cold water. When lukewarm, add 1 envelope dry yeast. After 5 minutes, stir.

Add 5-5½ cups flour. Knead 100 times on a lightly floured board. Let rise 1-1½ hours.

Punch down and shape into 2 loaves. Place on greased cookie sheet. Pull hard to lengthen loaves. Let rise 1 hour.

Slash top and brush with beaten egg whites. Bake for 10 minutes at 425°, then for 30 minutes at 300°.

BARBEQUED CHICKEN

Though you might not believe it on first reading, the ingredients listed in this recipe are correct—
John Wherry, Funeral Director
Pawnee City, NE

1 cut up chicken
1 cup catsup
1 can Pepsi

Place raw chicken in pieces in electric skillet. Mix catsup and Pepsi. Pour over chicken. Simmer in skillet for 3 to 4 hours.

WDO: John Wherry is (among other things) in the funeral biz. Neither the chicken nor his clients have complained about this recipe.

General John T. Chain, Jr.—just one more shrimp...

Rep. Doug Bereuter enjoys (?) an in-office gourmet meal.

Milan Bish (LOVE the shirt!).

Father Val Peter among friends—but then he always is.

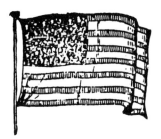

NATIONAL NOTABLES WASHINGTON AND OTHERWISE

One advantage of being married to a Governor is the opportunity it provides to meet National Notables. Not being shy, I asked most of them to contribute to the cookbook. What follows are some interesting recipes from some very interesting people...some with special Nebraska ties, some without.

SPANISH CHICKEN

Ambassador and Mrs. Walter Annenberg
Rancho Mirage, CA

8 tbsp. butter
3 lb. chicken pieces
1 large green pepper, chopped
1 large onion, chopped
1 15 oz. can whole tomatoes
1 10½ oz. can tomato puree
1½ cups chicken broth
2 tbsp. sugar
oregano
thyme
cumin
salt and pepper
½ lb. button mushrooms
2 cups cooked small peas

Heat 4 to 6 tbsp. butter in large skillet, preferably one with an enameled or non-stick surface. Add chicken and brown well. Add green pepper and onion, saute, then add tomatoes, tomato puree, broth and sugar. Stir in seasonings. Cover and simmer until chicken is tender, about 30 to 40 minutes.

While chicken cooks, saute mushrooms in 2 tbsp. butter. Before serving, stir mushrooms and peas into chicken and heat through. Serves 4.

WDO: Annenbergs and Reagans have been long-time friends. The Ambassador and his wife were among the guests at Reagan's final State dinner honoring Margaret Thatcher, to which Kay and I were also invited. We treasure both that experience and this recipe.

CHICKEN BAKE

The secret ingredient that makes this "ordinary" baked chicken "out of this world"? Just before eating, cover each serving with Tabasco.

Lee Atwater, Chairman
Republican National Committee, Washington, D.C.

---

4 chicken breasts
1 package chipped beef
1 can mushroom soup
1 carton sour cream
bacon

Skin and bone chicken breasts. Wrap each piece with 1 strip of bacon. Grease baking dish with butter. Cover bottom of dish with chipped beef. Arrange chicken on beef. Mix undiluted soup and sour cream and pour over chicken. Bake at 275° uncovered for 2-3 hours. Serves 4.

WDO: Lee was Campaign Chairman for President Bush and has since been named Chairman of the Republican National Committee. His Southern upbringing evidences itself with the generous use of the "secret ingredient".

PORK ROAST

Douglas Bereuter
U.S. House of Representatives, Washington, D.C.

1 pork loin boneless roast

Place roast in a pan (with a lid) and top with ONE of the following:

1 can Solo apricot filling or
1 can Solo prune filling or
1 can sauerkraut

Add potatoes and carrots later if desired. Topping will glaze pork and vegetables during baking. Bake at 325° for amount of time weight of roast requires.

CHICKEN
A LA REAGAN

This recipe was first used during a Presidential visit to Barbados on April 8, 1982, when I was U.S. Ambassador to the Eastern Caribbean.

Milan Bish
Grand Island, NE

---

2 chicken breasts split (4 pieces total- about 1½ lbs.)
½ cup flour
½ tsp. salt
¼ tsp. pepper
¼ cup vegetable oil
¼ cup rum
½ cup crushed pineapple in natural juice
¾ cup orange juice
¼ cup seedless raisins
¼ tsp. ground cinnamon
1/8 tsp. ground cloves
2 tbsp. butter
¼ cup blanched slivered almonds

Rinse chicken, pat dry. Combine flour, salt and pepper. Dredge chicken thoroughly, shaking off excess flour. Heat oil over moderate heat in heavy skillet. Brown chicken pieces on all sides until golden. Place chicken pieces in shallow pan. Combine rum, pineapple, orange juice, raisins, cinnamon and cloves. Pour mixture over chicken. Bake uncovered at 350° for 1 hour, 30 minutes, basting frequently.

In a small saucepan, melt the butter. Add the almonds and saute over moderate heat until golden. Pour the almonds and butter over the chicken . Serve with rice. Serves 4.

❧

WDO: Kay and I had the privilege of visiting Milan and Allene in Barbados. The food they served was as beautiful as the country in which he was serving as Ambassador.

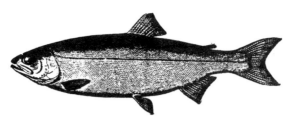

NOVA SCOTIA MOUSSE

Charlie and I both tend to cook for guests together...and we like recipes that can be prepared ahead so entertaining can still be done during a busy campaign season. Hope you enjoy these two favorites.

Judy A. and Charles R. Black
Washington, D.C.

Sprinkle 1 envelope unflavored gelatin onto ¼ cup cold water. Dissolve mixture in ½ cup hot light cream, then cool.
Mash together until smooth:

---

8 oz. cream cheese at room temperature
1 cup sour cream
1 tsp. Worcestershire sauce
¼ tsp. hot pepper sauce
1 clove garlic, mashed
2 tbsp. chopped chives

Stir all above ingredients into dissolved gelatin.
Add:

---

1 tsp. lemon juice (fresh)
1 tbsp. chopped parsley
1 tbsp. white horseradish
½ lb. Nova Scotia salmon
¼ cup chopped black olives (optional)

Fold in:

---

4 oz. red salmon caviar

Pour into well-greased 3 cup mold. Refrigerate. Can be served with crackers or sliced avocado and lemon.

CHOCOLATE, CHOCOLATE PIE

Judy A. and Charles R. Black
Washington, D.C.

1 cup undiluted evaporated milk
1 cup semi-sweet chocolate morsels
⅓ cup sugar
2 egg yolks
8 oz. cream cheese, cubed
graham cracker crust
whipped cream for topping

Place ½ cup milk in ice cube tray or pan and freeze until ice crystals form. Heat remaining ½ cup milk. Put chocolate chips and hot milk in blender. Whirl, adding egg yolks one at a time; whirl, add cream cheese cubes. Keep whirling. Add ice milk last. Pour into crust and cover. Refrigerate a few hours. Garnish with whipped cream (add ½ cup amaretto to cream if you enjoy chocolate cherries!)

WDO: Judy and Charles were members of the White House staff and have made us feel "at home" during our visits to Washington, D.C. and other locations throughout the United States.

GINGER COOKIES
FOR CHRISTMAS

For over forty years our Christmas tree has been decorated with homemade cookies carefully wrapped and tied to the tree with big bows. George and I put our tree up well before Christmas. When our children were young, they would cut and eat a cookie a day from the tree. At the end of the cookies...Christmas was here!

Barbara Bush, First Lady
Washington, D.C.

½ cup Crisco
½ cup sugar
½ cup molasses
1½ tsp. vinegar
1 egg, beaten
3 cups sifted enriched flour
½ tsp. baking soda
½ tsp. cinnamon
½ tsp. ginger
¼ tsp. salt

Bring shortening, sugar, molasses, and vinegar to a boil. Cool. Add egg. Sift dry ingredients together, add to first mixture. Mix well and chill.

On a lightly floured surface, roll to 1/8″ for thin cookies. Cut into desired shapes and place on greased cookie sheet. Bake in a moderate oven at 375⁰ for 8-12 minutes. Cool for 5 minutes.

❧

WDO: George and Barbara Bush were a little busy last fall when I was collecting recipes. However, he always found time to inquire about the book's progress and she found time to send a recipe and some comments. History will decide what kind of President George has been. However, I predict Barbara will be one of the outstanding First Ladies ever. We have been to their home on more than one occasion and have always felt warmly welcomed.

FAST HORS D'OEUVRES

I first put this one together out of available ingredients one night when I received only 40 minutes notice that then-candidate Ronald Reagan and Nancy were coming to my house for dinner.

> *Robert Gray, Chairman*
> *Hill & Knowlton*
> *Washington, D.C.*

Take sliced whole wheat or oat bread, cut off crusts. Spread with Hellman's Mayonnaise mixed with chopped onions. Brown in broiler, cut into quarters.

❦

CAPITAL CHILI

This recipe won the cookoff contest in Washington one year.

2 lbs. lean ground beef
1 medium green pepper, diced
1 large or 2 small onions, diced
salt and pepper to taste
1 tsp. chili powder (or to taste)
3 cans kidney beans
1 large can tomatoes
1 medium can tomato sauce
1 tbsp. sugar

Brown beef in skillet with peppers, salt, pepper and onion. Drain fat, remove to large cooking pot. Add beans, tomatoes, tomato sauce and sugar. Cover and cook over low heat for 1½-2 hours, stirring frequently. Add water (up to one cup) if sauce is too thick. Serves 6.

❦

WDO: Bob is a native Nebraskan and one of the public relations industry's most influential people. We are proud of him and he is proud to claim his Nebraska heritage. The new communications center at Hastings College is named for him and was personally dedicated by his close friend, Ronald Reagan.

LOUISE'S CHOCOLATE CAKE

Bob Kerrey, U.S. Senator
Washington, D.C.

1 cup butter or Crisco
2 cups sugar
2 eggs
2½ cups flour
1 tsp. salt
2 tsp. soda
½ cup cocoa
1 cup buttermilk
1 tsp. vanilla
1 cup boiling water

Cream butter and sugar. Add eggs. Sift dry ingredients and add to creamed mixture. Mix well. Add buttermilk, vanilla and boiling water. Mix well. Grease and flour a 9x13 pan. Bake at 375° for 35 minutes. Test with a toothpick for doneness.

Frost with a powdered sugar almond-flavored frosting.

❧

WDO: This guy was involved in a campaign at the time we were asking for recipes. You would have thought he would've just called one of his restaurants and had them send a recipe. Instead, he chose to share a sentimental favorite. Nice.

MONKEY BREAD

A fancy, ring-shaped bread that is a holiday favorite of ours.
Nancy Reagan, Former First Lady
Los Angeles, CA

1 package dry yeast
1 to 1¼ cups milk
3 eggs
3 tbsp. sugar
1 tsp. salt
3½ cups flour
6 oz. butter at room temperature
½ lb. melted butter
2 9-inch ring molds

In bowl, mix yeast with part of milk until dissolved. Add 2 eggs, beat. Mix in dry ingredients. Add remaining milk a little at a time, mixing thoroughly. Cut in butter until blended. Knead dough, let rise 1 to 1½ hours until double in size. Knead again, let rise 40 minutes.

Roll dough onto floured board, shape into a log. Cut log into 28 pieces of equal size. Shape each piece of dough into a ball and roll in melted butter. Use half of the pieces in each buttered, floured mold. Place 7 balls in each mold, leaving space in between. Place remaining balls "on top" of spaces. Let dough rise in mold. Brush tops with remaining egg. Bake in preheated oven at 375° until golden brown, approximately 15 minutes.

WDO: On more than one occasion, Kay and I have been honored to dine at the White House. One of the most memorable times for me was sitting next to Nancy Reagan at the spouses' luncheon held in conjunction with the National Governors' Association. Nancy is a tiny person, but a powerful one at the same time. She is absolutely devoted to her husband and brought an unquestioned measure of grace and elegance to The White House.

CANDIDATE'S CATFISH

Haven is such a great cook that I have a hard time finding anything good on the menu in the House of Representatives dining room.

Virginia (Mrs. Haven) Smith
U.S. House of Representatives
Washington, D.C.

Wash and dry fish with paper towel.

Sprinkle both sides with bay leaf seasoning, lemon pepper and generous portion of fresh garlic.

Slip into plastic bag, add ½ cup white wine. Marinate all day, turning once.

Microwave at 50%, turning once, about 15 minutes total.

WDO: Virginia's idea of a close election is when she gets less than 85% of the vote. She and Haven are inseparable...and it's no wonder she brags about his cooking. This is a GREAT idea and I'll bet it would work with other kinds of fish, too.

SOUR CREAM
COFFEE CAKE

This is mouth-watering served warm from the oven.
John (and Nancy) Sununu
Chief of Staff, Bush Administration
Washington, D.C.

½ cup butter
1 cup sugar

Place in mixer bowl—beat. When mixed, add:

2 eggs
1 cup sour cream
1 tsp. vanilla
2 cups flour
1 tsp. baking soda
1 tsp. baking powder
½ tsp. salt

Pour into tube pan, sprinkle in between layers a mix of 1 tsp. cinnamon to ½ cup sugar. (You can also add chopped nuts). Save some to put on the top.

Bake at 325° for 50 minutes.

SWEET AND SOUR MEATBALLS

John (and Nancy) Sununu
Chief of Staff, Bush Administration
Washington, D.C.

3 lbs. hamburger
2 eggs
3 tsp. Worcestershire sauce
3 tsp. salt
1 tsp. pepper
2 tsp. marjoram
1 tsp. prepared mustard
1 tsp. garlic salt
1 tsp. onion salt
½ cup Pepperidge Farm stuffing

Mix and roll into small meatballs. Brown with 1 package frozen chopped onions. Add:

1 lg. can tomatoes
¾ cup lemon juice
¾ cup brown sugar

Let simmer for 1 hour and serve warm.

WDO: The Sununus have 8 children. You don't need to worry whether either of their recipes is good...they've had a lot of practice feeding people! When we first met Sununus, he was Governor of New Hampshire. With my help and Kay's advice, he is now Chief of Staff in the Bush administration. Kay and I take much of the credit.

DUSTY SUNDAE

Warren Buffett, Chairman, Berkshire Hathaway Inc.
Omaha, NE

My ideas about food and diet were irrevocably formed quite early—the product of a wildly successful party that celebrated my 5th birthday. On that occasion we had hot dogs, hamburgers, soft drinks, popcorn and ice cream.

I found complete gastronomical fulfillment in this array and have seen no reason subsequently to expand my horizons. In fact, I am thought to be so expert in this specialized area of food preparation that I am often called upon to act as a consultant for pre-puberty dinner parties. The loudest applause at such affairs is invariably rendered when I sculpt my "Dusty" Sundae.

This sophisticated-sounding delicacy is really quite simple in preparation: First pour generous quantities of Hershey's Chocolate Syrup over vanilla ice cream, and then build a mountain of malted milk powder atop the chocolate.

The caloric consumption produced by this concoction is inconsequential. Assume that your basal metabolism rate is 2800 calories per day. Simple arithmetic tells us that you can—indeed you must—consume slightly over 1 million calories per year. In my own case—with a life expectancy of about 25 years—this means that, in order to avoid premature death through starvation, I need to eat some 25 million calories. Why not get on with it?

WDO: In addition to writing a great letter, which is reproduced here, Warren also writes Berkshire Hathaway's annual report. It should be required reading for every school student, not only to gain from Warren's vast business experience, but to experience what power can be put into words when the author is as skilled as he.

TUNA SURPRISE

Johnny Carson, Entertainer
Burbank, CA

Go to the market.

Purchase one 6-½ oz. can of tuna.

Upon returning home, open the can using either an electric can opener or the old-fashioned hand opener.

Place the lid to one side.

Turn the can rapidly upside down, depositing the contents on a 10" white china plate.

Rinse can thoroughly as it can be used as an attractive centerpiece with the addition of a small bouquet of flowers.

You may now consume the tuna using the utensil of your choice.

Surprise! That's all there is...

WDO: The First Gentleman called Johnny Carson's secretary. The conversation follows:

F.G.: Would you please have Johnny send a recipe for the First Gentleman's Cookbook?

SEC: He doesn't do that sort of thing.

F.G.: I am not calling from Ohio or Vermont—this is Nebraska and it's Johnny's home state.

SEC: I don't care—he doesn't do that sort of thing.

F.G.: Would you please give Johnny the request as follows (I had her read it back).

SEC: OK, I'll do that.

F.G.: And besides, I don't want Johnny to be embarrassed when I am on the Tonight Show and he doesn't have a recipe in the book.

The next weekend, Johnny and his family were in Norfolk, NE to dedicate the Carson Radiology Center. It was built in memory of Johnny's parents, with a large portion of the funds coming from Johnny personally. The First Gentleman accompanied Governor Kay Orr to the dedication, where he met Johnny, who said, "And YOU want a recipe for your cookbook." (Obviously, the message had gotten through.)

The following Friday, the NEW YORK TIMES did a half page article on the First Gentleman's Cookbook. A few days later, Johnny's Executive Secretary called me to discuss a "possible appearance on the Tonight Show." Resisting the temptation to say, "I don't do that sort of thing," I talked with her further and hope to make such an appearance once the book is available.

Anyway, Johnny's recipe is included and he characterizes it, as a "gag" recipe. I don't know whether that means one might "gag" on the results—or it is, in fact, a Johnny Carson "gag". I suspect the latter.

MOLASSES COOKIES

These always remind me of the big cookies you'd see in the comic strips—particularly the Katzenjammer Kids, who often had big molasses cookies on the windowsill. I love the smell of these baking when you come in from outdoors.

Dick Cavett, Entertainer
New York, NY

Mix:
¾ cup melted oleo
¾ cup brown sugar
1 egg
¼ cup dark molasses

Sift together:
2 ¼ cups flour
2 tsp. soda
½ tsp. cloves
1 tsp. ginger
1 tsp. cinnamon

Stir dry ingredients into molasses mixture and chill several hours. Then form balls and place on lightly greased cookie sheet. Flatten with fork dipped in cold water. Bake at 350° for 12-15 minutes.

❧

WDO: Dick Cavett's unique sense of humor has its roots in Nebraska. It's interesting to note how this kind of wit "sells" on both coasts...along with some of our other positive midwestern qualities. Dick has been generous with his support of the soon-to-be finished Lied Center for the Performing Arts in Lincoln. As Honorary Chairman, he has literally "put his money where his mouth is", providing both financial help and valuable Lied-ership.

GRAVLAX ON WHOLE WHEAT PUMPERNICKEL

Special instructions: Go to Labrador, Canada. Catch a 4-5 lb. salmon using a fly rod and wet fly. Then...
General John T. Chain, Jr.,
Chief, Strategic Air Command
Omaha, NE

1 piece of salmon, 4-5 lbs., cut in half and boned;
leave skin on
¼ cup coarse salt
¼ cup sugar
2 tbsp. peppercorns (preferably white),
crushed or coarsely ground
2 large bunches dill
2 loaves whole wheat pumpernickel, thinly sliced
Mustard Sauce:
4 tbsp. dijon mustard
1 tsp. dry mustard
3 tbsp. sugar
2 tbsp. white vinegar
⅓ cup light vegetable oil
1 small bunch dill, finely chopped

To cure salmon: put half the fish, skin side down, in a glass dish. Combine the salt, sugar and pepper and sprinkle on the fish, covering the whole side. Spread the dill over the seasonings. Put the other half of the salmon over the dill, skin side up. Cover with plastic wrap. Put a smaller dish on top of the salmon and weight it down with a heavy object. Refrigerate for 3-4 days. Turn the salmon every day.

To make sauce: combine mustards, sugar and vinegar in a bowl or food processor. Add the oil drop by drop until the mixture is thick. Stir in the dill. Refrigerate until ready to use, up to 3 or 4 weeks.

To serve: remove fish from the marinade. Wipe clean and pat dry. Slice each side on the diagonal into thin pieces, much as you would smoked salmon. Serve on half slices of whole wheat bread, topped with the sauce.

Premake and serve on platter: serves 50.

❧

WDO: As head of the Strategic Air Command based in Omaha, Jack has assumed an important leadership role in our state. Jack and Judy have hosted the Governor and me in their home on more than one occasion—the food and the fellowship are unforgettable.

SHARON'S
STILTON SAUCE

Wonderful over filets or sirloin. Excellent sauce choice for dinner parties. (Ed. Note: Made this for Christmas Eve "Eve" over beef tenderloin and it was exceptional. Froze what was left over and used it later—just as good as the first time.)
Chip Davis, Composer/Director, Mannheim Steamroller
Omaha, NE

Melt 3 tbsp. butter in saucepan
add 3 tbsp. flour and mix well
add 2 cans (16 oz.) beef consomme
slowly to avoid lumps
add 1 can (8 oz.) beef boullion
Simmer 1½-2 hours until reduced by ½
Add ¼ to ½ cup crumbled stilton cheese (to taste)
Add ¼ to ½ cup port wine (to taste)

Stir well and heat to serving temperature.

WDO: This fellow is, indeed, a breath of "Fresh Aire". He is the creative composer and leader of Mannheim Steamroller. Even though Chip could live anywhere, he has chosen to stay in Nebraska and thrives on the creative environment of our state. He also contributes greatly in return. As usual, his Christmas Concert in Omaha was sold out and sensational.

ARMENIAN SALAD

Gloria Deukmejian, First Lady, State of California
Sacramento, CA

Mix together in a salad bowl:
4 cups tomatoes in bite-size pieces
⅔ to 1 cup green pepper in bite-size pieces
½ cup parsley, snipped
½ cup scallions, sliced
2 sliced cucumbers
¼ cup lemon juice
2 tsp. salt

Toss and serve immediately. Serves 6.

WDO: George and Gloria are rightfully proud of their Armenian heritage and present a recipe which reflects that. It's also easy, colorful and nutritious—how can you beat that?

SPINACH DIP

Quick to fix and always quick to disappear when we entertain guests at the Mansion.

Margie Goldschmidt, First Lady
State of Oregon
Salem, OR

---

1 package frozen chopped spinach
½ cup chopped parsley
½ cup chopped green onions
½ tsp. dill weed
1 tsp. salad supreme
1 cup mayonnaise
1 cup sour cream
juice of one lemon

Thaw and squeeze out the spinach. Mix with all ingredients and refrigerate for several hours to allow flavors to blend. Serve with your choice of crackers.

WDO: A "First Lady" from the Pacific Northwest provides us with one of her favorite hors d'oeuvres.

BROWNIES

Katharine Hepburn, Actress
A Small Town in Connecticut

8 oz. unsweetened chocolate
2 cups butter

Add and mix by hand vigorously:

2 tsp. vanilla
8 eggs
4 cups sugar
1 tsp. salt

Add and mix by hand vigorously again:

1 cup flour

Bake at 340° for 30-40 minutes.

WDO: This one came to me by way of The Garden Cafe in Omaha. I don't really know if it's hers, but the instructions sound like her. She doesn't seem the "electric mixer" type. If the brownies are as fantastic as her acting...they've gotta be good.

NOEL CHICKEN

If you have as many mouths to feed as I do and want to have a fancy dinner—try this one:
Father Val J. Peter, Executive Director, Boys Town
Omaha, NE

6 medium chicken breasts
3 oz. can broiled mushrooms
1 can cream of mushroom soup
1 cup sour cream
½ cup sherry

First: catch some chickens. Make sure they are medium (the big ones are too tough and the little ones are too fast to catch). Remove all of the feathers (if you like to eat feathers, serve them as a side dish).

Place chicken breasts, skin side up, in an 11½ x 7½ x 1½ baking dish. Combine remaining ingredients, including mushroom juice; pour over chicken breasts. Sprinkle generously with paprika. Bake in moderate oven (350°) for 1¼ hours until done. Meanwhile, you can clean the kitchen—it's going to be an awful mess with all those feathers.

WDO: Father Val Peter's cherubic good looks (see page 162), good humor and positive outlook have helped make Boys Town the great institution it is. He was once quoted in the USA TODAY newspaper as follows:

"Anyone can sit and look at the seashore and be inspired because it shouts at you. So do the mountains. But the prairie only whispers. You must listen closely and never miss the message."

With credit to him, it is a quote I use often to describe to friends in other parts of the country and abroad the unique appeal of "Beautiful Nebraska".

MY FAVORITE RECIPE

Tiny Tim
Entertainer

Raw sunflower seeds

Open Pit BBQ Sauce (very important it be this brand for best flavor combination)

Put #2 on top of #1.

WDO: This guy is something else! He was appearing in Lincoln and we were introduced while he was on a radio talk show. I wouldn't tiptoe through the tulips—or anywhere else—to try this recipe. I think it sounds just awful. But then...to each his own.

JOHN WAYNE'S CHEESE CASSEROLE

Ed. Note: I saw "the Duke" make this on a television show many years ago. It was reported to be his "favorite" food. I have made it many times since—always to any cheese-lover's pleasure.

---

2 4-oz. cans of chopped green chilis, drained
1 lb. each monterey jack and cheddar, grated
4 egg whites
4 egg yolks
⅔ cup canned evaporated milk
1 tbsp. flour
½ tsp. salt
1/8 tsp. pepper
2 sliced tomatoes

Preheat oven to 325°. Put cheese and chilis in greased dish. Beat egg whites. Mix rest of ingredients in separate bowl. Fold in egg whites. Slide gently into baking dish and "ooze" cheese/chili mixture through it. Bake 30 minutes. Remove and arrange tomato slices around edge. Bake 1/2 hour more.

🌳

WDO: We added this one...after all, we already had Katharine Hepburn...and who else could match her magnitude but John Wayne?

CFBA
(CLOSE FRIENDS AND BUSINESS ASSOCIATES)
WOODMEN AND OTHERWISE

For almost thirty years, I have been associated with Woodmen Accident and Life of Lincoln, Nebraska. First joining the company in Illinois, I moved to Nebraska on a "temporary" basis some 25 years ago. One is blessed when he can find a successful company which also includes business associates who can at the same time be considered friends. Also included in this group are other friends some of whom are in the insurance business and some of whom are not. Since our industry is so fraught with initials (CLU, ChFP, LIMRA, LUTC, HIQA, etc. etc.), I couldn't resist titling this chapter in the same fashion. Real question is—why don't we just call it Alphabet Soup?

HAWAIIAN PORK CHOPS

This is the recipe that won the Pork Division of the 1987 Journal-Star recipe contest.
Brent Adams, Systems Programmer
Woodmen Accident and Life, Lincoln, NE

18 oz. can sliced pineapple
¾ cup teriyaki sauce
1 tbsp. Worcestershire sauce
3 tbsp. lemon juice
3 tbsp. apple juice
¼ cup brown sugar
¼ cup honey
4 to 6 pork chops, 1 inch thick

Drain pineapple, reserving juice. Combine pineapple juice with remaining ingredients except pork chops. Mix until brown sugar is dissolved. Marinate pork chops overnight in covered dish. Broil over medium-low heat for 12 to 15 minutes on each side. Place pineapple ring and 1 tsp. sauce on top of each chop for last 5 minutes of broiling time.

WDO: To the outside world, Brent is a computer programmer. Privately, he is an aspiring chef who has established some degree of credibility by winning a local cooking contest. Just so he doesn't get his bytes mixed up with his bites.

CLARK'S "CAHUETE" CONCOCTION*

C. W. Faulkner, Chairman (retired)
Woodmen Accident and Life
Lincoln, NE

Carefully slice two pieces of frozen seven grain whole wheat bread, approximately one quarter inch thick. Set aside and allow to come to room temperature for at least thirty minutes. While waiting, ready the following ingredients:

1½ tbsp. freshly ground natural peanut butter
1¾ tbsp. homemade mayonnaise
3 well-washed leaves of crisp head lettuce (3 x 3½")

When it is time to assemble this sandwich, juxtapose the two pieces of bread. Spread the peanut butter on both slices of bread evenly and generously.

Now place the three leaves of lettuce on the left hand slice and cover the right hand slice with mayonnaise. Gingerly place the two pieces together and press lightly with the left hand to blend the flavors. Do not slice. Serve immediately. Voila!

❦

WDO: This man was my boss for more than 25 years. He is a good friend and an outstanding yachtsman. (In WWII he won the Navy Cross as a PT Boat Commander.) Even though Clark has traveled extensively throughout the world, he has never developed a taste for exotic foods. Therefore it is only appropriate that we share his famous peanut butter sandwich recipe with the world.

* This is the one that started the peanut butter controversy. See page 281.

CHICKEN BREASTS SUPREME

Aspirants to high public office whose campaigns involve endless exposure to bountiful banquets and the fat of the land generally think highly of this recipe. Whether the centerpiece of a brunch, luncheon or dinner, this dish is light and tasty, but satisfying. Complemented with a dry white wine, toasted English muffins and orange marmalade, it is equally pleasing to gentle lady and giant "hunk." It was originally created by Rose M. Bingham, Cateress.

E.J. Faulkner, Honorary Chairman,
Woodmen Accident and Life
Lincoln, NE

3 chicken breasts, skinned, deboned and split
½ cup flour
1 tsp. paprika
2 tsp. dried onion flakes
⅓ cup melted butter or margarine
2 cans cream of mushroom soup
1 tsp. Worcestershire sauce
1 tsp. Accent
1 tsp. coarse ground pepper
1 cup milk or half and half

Coat the chicken breasts in flour/paprika mixture. Put dried onion flakes inside each breast piece and roll up. Put folded side down into melted butter or margarine. Spoon some of the butter over each piece to coat, add any leftover onion flakes. After lightly browned, pour a sauce consisting of the soup, Worcestershire sauce, Accent, ground pepper (add no salt) and half and half over the breasts and put in the oven to bake at 325° for one hour.

If sauce is too thick, thin with more milk or half and half. If browning too much, put a lid over it. Test for tenderness.

Serve over wild rice or wild and white rice mixed together. Or over noodles. Pass remaining gravy to be added by those who wish. Serves 6.

❦

WDO: Woody Varner has described E.J. as "The Big 8 Champion of the Verbal Bench Press." Who else would start a sentence with "aspirants"? E.J. has had a profound influence on Kay and me through his active involvement in Republican politics and his many decades of leadership in the insurance industry.

LOUISIANA SHRIMP

After you start dunking the bread, don't forget the shrimp!
Jeff Freed, Agency Vice President
Woodmen Accident and Life
Lincoln, NE

¾ cup butter
1 bay leaf
¼ cup fresh lemon juice
1 tsp. garlic powder
1 tsp. cayenne
1½ tsp. lemon pepper
½ cup water
1 pound raw shrimp

Place all ingredients but shrimp in a pot and heat until butter melts. Place shrimp in one layer in an ovenproof shallow glass dish. Pour butter mixture over shrimp and bake at 350° for 40 minutes. Serve at the table from the glass dish with PLENTY of french bread for dunking in the butter sauce. To be shared with close friends. Serves 4.

WDO: Jeff keeps an eye on the Western Division of Woodmen's agency operations. His recipe has been tried by several who claim it to be one of the best shrimp dishes around.

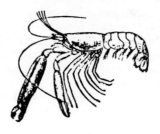

GIN'S BAR COOKIES

Good and easy. A favorite during my Campfire leader and PTA days, but adults like them, too. Forget about the calories. I adhere to the saying, "Life is uncertain; eat dessert first!".
Mrs. John (Nancy) Haessler, Wife of the President
Woodmen Accident and Life
Lincoln, NE

½ cup sugar
½ cup light corn syrup
¾ cup peanut butter
3 cups Special K cereal
6 oz. package chocolate chips
6 oz. package butterscotch chips

Lightly butter a 9″ square pan. In saucepan, bring sugar and syrup to a boil, stirring frequently. Remove from heat and stir in peanut butter, then cereal. Press mixture into pan. Melt chocolate and butterscotch chips over hot water. Spread over top of cereal mixture. Cool and cut into bars.

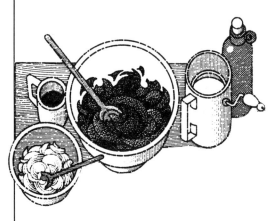

CHICKEN EN CASSEROLE

An ideal company casserole; no last-minute fuss. A most requested entree for family celebrations. Everyone likes it. With this recipe, I don't have to remember which daughter abhors broccoli and which one loves it.

Mrs. John (Nancy) Haessler, Wife of the President
Woodmen Accident and Life
Lincoln, NE

---

5 boned chicken breasts, cut in half
1 box Uncle Ben's Long Grain and Wild Rice mix
1 can cream of chicken soup
1 can cream of mushroom soup
1 can cream of celery soup
½ cup milk
¼ cup melted butter
½ cup sauterne wine
5 oz. can of sliced water chestnuts, drained
3 oz. can broiled sliced mushrooms, drained
2 tbsp. chopped green pepper
2 ¼ oz. package of shaved almonds
3 oz. freshly grated Parmesan cheese

Grease 9x13 pyrex pan. Put in raw rice. Mix soups with melted butter, milk, wine, water chestnuts, mushrooms and green pepper. Pour small amount of mixture on top of rice. Layer chicken breasts and add rest of mixture. Sprinkle almonds and parmesan cheese on top. Bake covered at 275° for 2 hours. Uncover and bake ½ hour longer. Do not touch during baking. Serves 8-10.

❦

WDO: Everyone in my company evenutally reports to President John Haessler...who eventually reports to Nancy Haessler. Now you know the rest of the story.

MEATBALLS CON QUESO

For a very hearty meal, you can serve this over cornbread. For dip, serve with chips.

Ralph Kellison, 2nd Vice President
Woodmen Accident and Life
Lincoln, NE

For meatballs:
1½ lbs. ground beef
⅓ cup chopped onion
½ cup dry oatmeal
1 egg

Shape mixture into 1 inch balls...in 10 inch skillet, over medium high heat cook meatballs a few at a time in 3 tbsp. hot salad oil. Cook until browned and drain on paper towels.

For use in dip:
1½ lbs. ground beef browned, crumbled and drained on paper towels.

For Sauce:

Pour grease from skillet and wipe with a paper towel. Into skillet over low heat, stir 16 oz. Velveeta cheese cubed, 4 oz. chopped green chilis with liquid, 1 package taco seasoning mix and ¾ cup water. Mix and cook until cheese is melted.

Return meatballs (for meal) or crumbled meat (for dip) to the sauce and heat through. Keep warm in chafing dish or crockpot.

Chips: Heat ½″ salad oil in heavy skillet until hot but not smoking. Immerse fresh corn tortillas in hot oil one at a time for a few moments, turning frequently to avoid burning. When crisp, drain on paper towels and salt while still hot. When cool, break into chips.

❧

WDO: Ralph grows more chili peppers than anyone I know in the city of Lincoln. This recipe is the "most admired" dish every Christmas at Woodmen. It's dynamite in more ways than one!

HANGTOWN FRY

Reputedly, the Hangtown Fry was created during the California Gold Rush Days. Oysters and eggs were seldom-enjoyed delicacies craved by those gold miners who had "struck it rich" and could afford the most expensive items on the menu. In these cholesterol-conscious days, perhaps we also must consider this dish a delicacy to be enjoyed infrequently.
Dean Kirby, 2nd Vice President (retired)
Woodmen Accident and Life
Lincoln, NE

1 dozen fresh oysters
flour
9 eggs
fine cracker crumbs
3 tbsp.butter

Drain oysters and dip in flour seasoned with salt and pepper, then in well-beaten eggs and last in cracker crumbs. Saute in heated butter until lightly browned. Beat remaining eggs with salt and pepper. Pour over oysters and cook until firm on the bottom. Turn with large spatula and cook second side a minute or two longer. Serves 4.

WDO: Since Dean retired about a year ago, he has dedicated his time to good causes. He was a business associate of mine for more than 25 years and continues to be a good friend. Dean has bragged about this Hangtown Fry recipe for years.

JOE'S FAMOUS BAKED EGGS

Delicious and filling!

Joe Neal, Vice President/Marketing
Woodmen Accident and Life
Lincoln, NE

Lightly grease individual baking dishes.

Lay one slice of buttered whole wheat toast or ½ English muffin in bottom. Alternate two layers of either sliced Canadian bacon or Danish ham and Swiss cheese. Over two eggs, put 2-3 spoons of mixture made from:

---

4 tbsp. sour cream
1 tbsp. Durkee's Sauce (or to taste)
salt and pepper to taste

Sprinkle top lightly with Parmesan cheese and paprika. Bake uncovered at 350° approximately 15 minutes or until egg whites begin to set. Serve immediately.

WDO: Joe is Vice President/Marketing for Woodmen Accident and Life and a passionate chef. He has dedicated himself to keeping tradition alive in his family's kitchen.

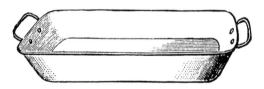

FANCY
MEATBALL DISH

More of an entree than an appetizer, but it could go either way.
Serve atop buttered noodles for the former, in a chafing dish
with cocktail picks for the latter.
Diane Payne, Assistant Vice President
Woodmen Accident and Life
Lincoln, NE

---

2 slices of bacon
1 tsp. (or 1 cube) instant beef boullion
1 cup boiling water
1 lb. ground beef
1 egg
¼ cup bread crumbs
½ tsp. salt
dash of pepper

Fry bacon until crisp; crumble and set aside, reserving drippings. Dissolve boullion in boiling water. Combine ¼ cup of beef broth with ground beef, egg, bread crumbs, salt and pepper; mix well. Shape meat mixture into small balls and brown in bacon drippings. Transfer meatballs into 1½ qt. casserole.

In same skillet, cook 2 thinly sliced medium onions until golden; spoon atop meatballs. Stir 2 tbsp. flour into bacon drippings; add remaining beef broth and ¾ cup beer. Stir in 1 tsp. brown sugar, 1 tsp. vinegar, ¼ tsp. salt, ¼ tsp. crushed dried thyme and a dash of pepper.

Cook and stir until mixture thickens and bubbles. Pour over onions and meatballs. Cover and bake in 350° oven for 45 minutes or longer. Top with 2 tbsp. snipped parsley and crumbled bacon just before serving. Serves four as a main dish.

❧

WDO: Diane has managed to run her department at Woodmen,
raise a family and stay good at cooking, too!

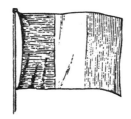

LASAGNE

I found this recipe years ago when I first started traveling. We have used it many times for entertaining and it has become one of our favorites.

Jeff Powell, Agency Vice President
Woodmen Accident and Life

¼ cup olive oil
2 medium onions
4 medium cloves garlic
4 lbs. lean ground beef
1 tbsp. oregano
3 tsp. salt
1 tsp. pepper
2 6-oz. cans tomato paste
2 8-oz. cans tomato sauce
1 cup dry red wine
1 lb. package lasagne noodles
2½ lb. ricotta cheese
1 lb. mozzarella cheese
12 heaping tbsp. grated Parmesan cheese

Heat olive oil in large heavy pot over medium heat. Add onions (finely chopped) and cloves of garlic (either put them through a press or mince). Stir frequently until they are golden. Add the ground meat, turn heat to high and brown it well. Add the oregano, salt and pepper and stir. Add the tomato paste, tomato sauce and wine, stir and turn heat down to low. Cover and cook for an hour or an hour and a half, stirring occasionally.

Put a 10 or 12 qt. pot of water on to boil, and add 2 tbsp. of salt. When the water is boiling, add the lasagne noodles without breaking them. Cook for about 20 minutes, stirring gently from time to time with a wooden spoon. Drain into a colander and, being careful not to burn your fingers, lay the noodles piece by piece on damp cloths.

Grease two 11 x 7 pyrex dishes with butter or margarine. Cover the bottom of one dish with the noodles, spread the meat sauce generously over them and cover with ricotta. (If the ricotta isn't creamy, put it in a large bowl, add 3 or 4 tbsp. of milk and beat with a spoon.) Repeat the process until you have used half of the ingredients, and over the last layer add

(continued)

half the mozzarella, sliced thin, and sprinkle with half the Parmesan cheese. Repeat the same process with the second dish.

Preheat the oven to 350°. Bake the lasagne for about 45 minutes to an hour (it should bubble). If you like, you may place it under the broiler to brown the top before serving.

With this, I serve french bread, wine and fried spinach with garlic. The fried spinach is really great. You just cook spinach, add salt, pepper and minced garlic to taste and fry it in butter.

❦

WDO: Jeff is a long-time associate at Woodmen. Believe it or not, he was a chef at one time and contributes a recipe from that period of his life.

TABOULI

This is a Lebanese salad that is best made during the summer growing season when the vegetables and mint can be picked fresh from the garden. It is easily modified to add a variety of vegetables and is a tasty and healthful salad alternative. The bulgur wheat has a chewy, nutlike flavor that enhances almost any meal.

*Mrs. Fred (Margaret) Rickers, Wife of
Senior Vice President, Woodmen Accident and Life
Lincoln, NE*

1½ cups bulgur wheat (soak 1-2 hours)
3-6 green onions, chopped
1 cup celery, chopped
1 bunch parsley, chopped
3 large tomatoes, chopped
¼ cup fresh chopped mint leaves
1 tsp. salt (optional)
½ cup light vegetable oil
½ cup lemon juice
(may add ½ cup chopped cucumbers or bell peppers according to vegetable supply and taste)

Drain and squeeze the water from the wheat. Chop all the vegetables and mint and add to the bulgur. Add salt if desired and mix lemon juice and oil and add to the mixture. Chill and serve. This tastes best after the flavors have been allowed to mix and keeps well for several days refrigerated. Serves 6.

WDO: This recipe is not only quite interesting, but quite good. Fred has the distinction of being a "recovering actuary". This is to say that at one time, he was a practicing actuary and is no longer "addicted" to such activity. Happily we are business associates and enjoy a good working relationship (along with occasional tastes of his wife's Tabouli!).

TUNA AND POTATO POUF

It takes two people to create a good meal—one to prepare it and the other to enjoy it.

Herm and Helen Wiebers, Sr. Vice President/Treasurer
Woodmen Accident and Life
Lincoln, NE

---

8 med. sized potatoes, peeled, cut in half; cover to boil in 4 qt. pan until tender.

In small skillet, saute 2 - 6½ oz. cans of tuna, partially drained of its packing water, and 2 tsps. dried minced onion.

Drain cooking water off potatoes; add 1 tbsp. oleo, 1½ tsps. salt and pepper to taste. Gradually, while whipping the potato mixture, add ½ cup warm milk. Potatoes should be moist—if not, add more milk.

Fold the tuna mixture into the potatoes and place into a slightly greased 2 qt. casserole dish. Dot top with pats of oleo. Sprinkle top with pepper or paprika.

Brown the potato/tuna mixture uncovered in a 350° oven for 10-15 minutes. Whipped potatoes will "pouf" up slightly to provide a light, lovely consistency. 6 generous servings.

WDO: Herm's ability to advise the Company on various investments has been proven over the years. He is so conservative, however, that he is hesitant to make a "long-term" projection as late as December 30. Overall, I prefer his form of conservatism to the brand of investment advice established by some who have been forced to take up full-time gardening.

QUAIL OR PHEASANT DINNER

This recipe assumes you know how to get the necessary ingredients, i.e., pheasant and/or quail. Since this assumption may be flawed, perhaps the first step may be to get a good English pointer, German shorthair or Brittany spaniel.

Jack Wood, Agency Vice President
Woodmen Accident and Life
Lincoln, NE

After skinning the birds, soak them in salt water for about two hours and then allow them to chill for another hour.

The quail should be left whole, but the pheasant cut up as you would a chicken. Roll the whole quail and cut up pheasant in flour until well coated. Season liberally with salt, pepper and poultry seasoning. Adding a small amount of sage really gives the birds a very delicate and unusual flavor.

Using a moderate amount of oil, brown the birds in a frying pan over medium heat, turning as necessary. This usually takes 15 minutes maximum.

Remove birds from the frying pan and place in roaster pan at 300° for 45 minutes. Remove pan from oven and pour cream of mushroom soup over the birds (one can is sufficient for 1 pheasant and 6 quail). Return birds to 350° oven for 20 minutes and they are ready.

Serve with rice pilaf and asparagus spears and you'll have an unusual and elegant dinner.

WDO: With the possible exception of Henry Cech, there is no one I know who shoots more pheasant and quail than Jack and Donna Wood. Combining my shooting "luck" and Jack's numbers, we come out very average.

TOM'S BAKED BEANS

Eleanor Adamson
Lincoln, NE

---

2 1-lb. cans Van Camp Pork & Beans
¾ cup brown sugar
1 tsp. dry mustard
6 slices of bacon, chopped
½ cup ketchup

Empty 1 can of beans into casserole; combine sugar and mustard and sprinkle half of it over beans. Top with other can of beans and sprinkle with rest of sugar/mustard mixture, chopped bacon and ketchup.

Bake uncovered in slow oven (325°) for 2½ hours. Serves 6-8.

WDO: Eleanor's husband, Tom, was a professional life insurance representative and personal friend of mine. He died a few years ago, leaving his wife Eleanor to head a family which includes some beautiful grandchildren. She volunteered Tom's recipe, and I'm glad.

SWEET MILK PANCAKES

Del Cross, Farmer/Rancher
Bloomfield, NE

In blender:
5 eggs, well-beaten
½ tsp. salt
pinch of sugar
½ cup flour—more or less
1½ cup milk—more or less

Preheat frypan (medium high). Use butter or margarine for nonstick surface. Pour layer of batter any size. Flip when lightly brown.

To serve, immediately spread with butter and layer of sugar, fold up and eat.

Other options: syrup, strawberries and whipped cream, etc.

Makes 10-12 plate-sized thin pancakes.

WDO: Del is a farmer/rancher friend from Knox County. He is the father of Natalie Cross, now Natalie Peetz, in the Governor's Office. Del is tough. You've got to be to survive Knox County winters. (Summers make up for it, however.)

SPINACH AND SCALLOP SOUP

This is an unusual soup, a smooth puree of spinach with sliced mushrooms and scallops suspended within it. Shelled prawns or small strips of Dover sole may be substituted for the scallops. It is best followed by a plain meat dish, either roasted or grilled.

Pennie Davis, Investor
Omaha, NE

12 oz. spinach
6 oz. small button mushrooms
1 oz. butter
3 tbsp. sunflower oil
8 oz. potatoes, sliced
1¾ pints hot light chicken stock
6 large scallops
¼ pint cream
salt and freshly ground pepper
2 tbsp. lemon juice

Remove the spinach stalks and wash the leaves. Then shake well, pat dry and tear into pices. Remove the mushroom stalks amd chop them; wipe the caps and set aside.

Heat the butter and half the oil in a heavy saucepan and cook the spinach leaves and mushroom stalks gently for 4-5 minutes, then add the potatoes and the stock, with salt and pepper to taste. Cover and let simmer for 20 minutes, then remove from the heat and leave to cool for 5-10 minutes.

Meanwhile, slice the mushroom caps and fry them for a few moments in the remaining oil, just until they start to soften, then drain off the cooking juices and set aside. Steam the scallops for 3-4 minutes, depending on size. Slice each scallop into 3 round slices, leaving the coral tongues intact.

When the soup has cooled, puree it in a food processor or pass through a sieve. Stir in the cream. Return it to the pan and reheat, adding salt, pepper and lemon juice to taste. Add the sliced mushrooms and scallops. Serve immediately in heated bowls. Serves 6.

❦

WDO: Pennie Davis' skill in the kitchen is legendary. An invitation to one of his dinner parties is an honor and an experience to be treasured...he keeps alive the tradition of good food, good conversation and good wine, as you can see by the menu reprinted here.

Menu

Spinach and Scallops Soup
Fish Terrine with Puree of Green Peas
Lemon Sorbet

Matanzas Chardonnay '86

Rack of Veal with Mustard Sauce
Vine Leaves with Rice
Baby Carrots and Turnips with Pea Pods
Red and Yellow Peppers

Chateau Prieure Lichine '78

Leaves and Flowers Salad
Chocolate Marquise in Coffee Sauce

Ch Lafaurie Peyraguey Sauternes '81

209

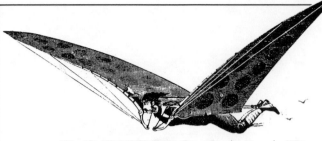

ROBERT'S SALAD AND DRESSING

This salad was created in the Spring of 1988. My family, and especially my husband, was never very enthusiastic about the greens I served. With this recipe, however, I had a winner and I dedicate it to my husband, Robert.

Karen Duncan, Wife of President, Duncan Aviation
Lincoln, NE

---

8 heads of butter lettuce—
washed, dried and broken into bite-sized pieces
2 bunches of green onions, cut up with tops included
1 bunch of fresh parsley—both men and children
think they don't like parsley, so it is necessary
to cut it very fine with scissors (stems NOT included)
1 cup raisins—I use Monnukka Raisins if possible;
I don't know why, but they're better.
1 cup slivered almonds

DRESSING:
½ cup sugar
½ cup white wine tarragon vinegar (use NO other!)
1 cup salad oil—Puritan is most healthy
2 tsp. salt
2 tsp. pepper

Mix these ingredients in advance and refrigerate. Toss over the salad just before serving. This recipe serves 10, but may be adjusted to any size.

❧

WDO: Duncan Aviation is famous the world over. Bob has capitalized on the unique geographic location of Nebraska and the unique qualities of the Nebraska work ethic to literally put Lincoln, Nebraska "on the map". Both Bob and Karen are great appreciators of good food and good music as evidenced by their dedication to the Lincoln Symphony and their fabulous "in home" music room. Postscript: we have tried this—it's great!

PAULINE'S ABSOLUTE BEST HOMEMADE ICE CREAM

This is a 25-year tradition with the Dye family on the 4th of July. I guarantee you, you'll be the hit of the party. And, it's easy!
Joe Dye, Automobile Dealer
North Platte, NE

6 large eggs
2 cups sugar
dash of salt
3 tbsp. pure vanilla extract
2 4-oz. bars of Baker's German Sweet Chocolate*
1 pint whipping cream
½ cup white creme de cocoa
half and half as needed

* green label

Beat eggs with sugar, add salt and vanilla. Break up chocolate in food processor with metal blade. Pulverize (terribly noisy!). After broken into small bits, add egg mixture, whipping cream and creme de cocoa.

Place mixture in 1 gallon container from a White Mountain electric ice cream freezer. Fill container with half and half until about 3 inches from top. Follow directions for freezer, using plenty of ice and rock salt. When freezer begins to labor, stop, drain off excess water, pull the dasher out of container being careful not to get salty ice in ice cream. Recover container and pack with ice and salt and serve in an hour. If there would happen to be any left over, it keeps well in the refrigerator freezer in an airtight Tupperware container.

❦

WDO: Pauline raised an "all male" family. In the process she became an excellent cook in terms of both quantity and quality. I think I'll try to be in North Platte next July 4th...I'd even volunteer to "crank" if necessary!

THE VERSATILE CASSEROLE

Here's a "quick to fix" item that is as comfortable at a ladies' luncheon as it is at a poker party. No matter what your social scene, this plays to rave reviews.
Jim Eaton, Vice President, Wilson Learning Corp.
Minneapolis, MN

8 oz. package thin noodles
1½ lbs. ground beef
1 clove garlic
16 oz. tomato sauce
salt and pepper to taste
16 oz. cottage cheese
8 oz. cream cheese
¼ cup sour cream
⅓ cup chopped onion
1 cup grated cheddar cheese

Cook noodles according to package directions. Brown beef and garlic, add tomato sauce and seasonings.

Blend first two cheeses, sour cream and onions. In greased 9 x 13 pan, put one half noodles, then cheese mixture, then remaining noodles. Cover with ground beef mixture and top with cheddar cheese. Bake at 350° for 30 minutes.

WDO: I admire Jim and Susan Eaton for several reasons, not the least of which is their ability to withstand the harsh winters and unforgiving freezes of Arrowhead Country. They are truly "warm" people.

SPARERIBS

This original recipe came from my great grandmother and called for covering the ribs with waxed brown paper. Since this is no longer available, we use aluminum foil. The soy sauce and steak sauce are also substitutes for ingredients no longer available.

Don A. Gorsline, 2nd Vice President
Life Insurance Marketing Research Ass'n
Hartford, CT

4 lbs. spareribs
Sauce:
1¼ cups light molasses
1 cup catsup
1 cup chopped onions
½ cup chopped celery
4 cloves of garlic, minced
6 whole cloves
juice of one orange
rind from ¼ orange, finely diced

2 tbsp. vinegar
2 tbsp. salad oil
1 tsp. prepared mustard
2 tbsp. soy sauce
½ tsp. salt
½ tsp. pepper
2 tbsp. Worcestershire sauce
½ tsp. Tabasco sauce
2 tbsp. margarine
2 tbsp. steak sauce

Place spareribs in shallow pan (I use oven broiler pan lined with wide heavy aluminum foil). Cover with foil. Roast for ½ hour at 325°. Drain off fat and turn ribs. Cover again and roast ½ hour longer. Meanwhile, prepare sauce by combining all ingredients, bring to a boil and let boil for 5 minutes. Let stand until ribs are ready for basting.

When ribs have roasted a second ½ hour, remove foil covering and drain off excess fat. Bring sauce to a boil again; pour over ribs. Raise oven heat to 400° and roast ribs uncovered for 25 minutes, basting often and turning after first 15 minutes. To serve, cut ribs into pieces with scissors and serve with a sweet and sour sauce.

❦

WDO: Don has been with LIMRA for as long as I can remember. His "research" extends over many years and as many free hotel meals as he could acquire in checking out possible future meeting sites.

BRIE EN PHYLLO

This is great served with wedges of Granny Smith apples. You can also serve it with pears.

Mrs. Tom (Ginny) Kelly
Wife of Sr. Vice President, LIMRA
Hartford, CT

---

8 sheets of phyllo pastry
2 sticks sweet butter
1 whole brie, not fully ripe (about 3 lbs.)
1 jar good quality apricot jam mixed
with ¼ cup brandy

Butter a quiche dish large enough to hold brie. Lay 4 sheets of phyllo on the dish, overlapping each other to cover bottom. Brush 1 stick of melted butter over dough. Set brie on top of pastry and cover with jam/brandy mixture. Fold up edges of phyllo around cheese. Cover top with other 4 sheets of pastry and brush with other stick of melted butter. Tuck edges under brie. Fold an additional sheet of phyllo in a 1 inch wide strip, roll to form a flower shape and center on top of cheese. Brush with butter. Bake for 20-30 minutes or until golden brown (350°). Let stand for at least 30 minutes before serving.

❧

WDO: To experience a cocktail buffet at Ginny's is every bit as good as being invited to the White House for a Black Tie Dinner. The above is just one example of the many exquisite dishes she prepares for such occasions.

GLAZED CORNISH HENS

A terrific party recipe—they can cook while cocktails are being served.

Elaine Macy, Regional Vice President, Maritz Travel
Tiburon, CA

1 can apricots
1 jar apricot jam or jelly
2-4 hens, cleaned
½ bottle white wine
1 can frozen orange juice
1 clove garlic
salt and pepper
margarine or butter

Cook hens, basted in melted butter with minced garlic, for 1½ hours at 350°. Stuff with recipe below.

While hens are cooking (or ahead of time if you have company) make glaze by mixing apricots, jelly, white wine and orange juice.

Last 30 to 45 minutes of cooking, baste hens with apricot mixture until glazed.

Stuffing:

1 box white and wild rice mixture (make according to package directions)

While rice is cooking, saute as many fresh sliced mushrooms, chopped onions and raisins as you would like to add to the stuffing. Add rice, splash with soy sauce and stuff hens.

WDO: This woman is NOT from Macy, Nebraska, although our State would be delighted to "claim" her. She lives in Tiburon, California (San Francisco) and represents Maritz Travel. To the insurance industry she IS Maritz Travel—a real professional! On special occasions she has served this to special friends who realize Elaine's hospitality extends to her home.

MEXI-CASSEROLE

Larry McNeese, Barber
Lincoln, NE

1½ lb. ground beef
1 package taco seasoning mix
(reserve 1 tsp. for topping)
10¾ oz. can condensed tomato soup
2 15 oz. cans chili beans or kidney beans

Topping:
1 cup Hungry Jack Buttermilk Extra Light
or Complete Pancake Mix
1 tsp. taco seasoning mix
1 cup shredded cheddar cheese
½ cup milk
1 tsp. parsley flakes

Preheat oven to 400°. Brown beef and drain. Stir in seasoning mix, soup and beans. Simmer while preparing topping.

Lightly spoon pancake mix into measuring cup and level off. Combine all topping ingredients and blend well.

Pour meat mixture into shallow 3 qt. casserole or 9 x 13 pan. Spoon topping over meat; sprinkle with parsley. Bake uncovered for 15-25 minutes until golden brown. Serve hot. Refrigerate any leftovers. Makes 8 one-cup servings.

May add green peppers, chilis and additional seasonings to taste.

WDO: Larry is my barber. That is an understatement. He is actually a part-time barber and a full-time chef. The annual wild game feed he puts on prior to Christmas is something that would cause most people to put up with very bad haircuts just to be eligible to attend. The good news is that Larry is not all that bad a barber.

STEAK TARTARE

The only way to make this is by using good lean meat with NO fat. Credit for the recipe goes to the chef at the Fairmont Hotel in New Orleans.

Larry Myers, President
Commercial Computer Systems
Lincoln, NE

1 lb. extra lean ground beef
2 tsp. Grey Poupon Dijon mustard
2 tsp. capers
¼ cup chopped onion
1 tbsp. olive oil
1 tbsp. red wine vinegar
4 anchovy fillets
juice of ½ lemon
chopped parsley for garnish
salt and pepper
½ tsp. Worcestershire sauce
1 egg yolk
Tabasco sauce to taste

To begin, put pepper and salt in a bowl (to your taste). Add capers, onions and anchovies and finely crush. Add lemon juice, mustard, Worcestershire sauce, egg yolk and Tabasco and mix.

Now add olive oil and wine vinegar and mix. Finally, add ground beef and toss till well blended.

Serve with melba toast or plain crackers.

WDO: Larry is the kind of guy who usually is hesitant about expressing an opinion or taking a position on a particular subject. Some of his friends, including yours truly, have been able to draw him out, and we find Larry has some pretty definite ideas on a number of subjects. Larry is in his "second" career, the first having been spent as a CPA.

FIVE CAN CASSEROLE

Actually, this recipe came from Mrs. Bertie C. Lyon and was published in the Tenessee Homecoming Cookbook, but I add Tabasco sauce. Does that make it "my" recipe?
Patricia N. Offer, Area Sales Manager, Sheraton Hotels
Honolulu, HI

1 small can boned chicken or turkey
1 small can evaporated milk
1 can cream of chicken soup
1 can cream of mushroom soup
1 5 oz. can Chinese noodles
Tabasco to taste

Mix all ingredients together. Bake in buttered casserole 25 minutes in a 350° oven or heat and serve from a chafing dish. It may be served plain or in pattie shells.

WDO: Pat was the first contributor of a recipe to this cookbook. Therefore, can we say this is a "First Offer"? She says this dish is "perfect for us last-minuters". Who, me?

PAN FRIED CHICKEN WITH GRAVY

A blow-by-blow account of how to come by this traditional favorite.

Ron Rapp, General Agent, New York Life
South Sioux City, NE

What you'll need:
large cast iron skillet
chicken parts you like (example: 6-8 legs or thighs
or 2-3 breasts—if you want to do more,
increase amounts shown in coating recipe)
medium size paper or plastic bag
outdoor gas grill with lid OR
be real neat on the stove
2 cup measuring cup

Coating:
put this stuff in the paper or plastic bag—
¾ cup regular flour
¼ cup fine corn meal
(if you don't have this skip it and increase the flour
or put some regular corn meal in the
blender or a coffee grinder)
spices—give or take measurements OR
leave out if you don't have
(put this stuff in the bag with the flour and corn meal)
½ tsp. paprika
¼ tsp. ground black pepper
¼ tsp. nutmeg
¼ tsp. thyme
¼ tsp. beau monde
½ tsp. dill weed
½ tsp. garlic powder OR 2 cloves fresh garlic
chopped up and put in the pan
before you cook the chicken
¼ tsp. curry powder
½ tsp. oregano
couple of shakes of seasoned salt—
pass if you don't want salt

(continued)

Put the chicken in a bowl and pour ½ cup regular milk over it—don't wash the measuring cup, you'll need it later.

Put enough solid shortening in the skillet to be about ½ inch deep when melted.

Mess the chicken around in the milk, pick it up, drain it a little, then put it in the sack. Shake it. Put excess milk back into the measuring cup.

Take the sack to the skillet and put the chicken into the hot oil—fry both sides until brown.

Put excess coating from the bag into the milk and add water up to 2 cup level. Use wire whisk to make a paste—don't worry about how thick it is—we'll add water later.

When chicken is about ½ done, take it out of the skillet and put it on the grill to finish cooking.

Pour almost all of the oil we've been cooking in off carefully—the skillet is HOT.

Put skillet back on grill and let it get hot again. Have 3 cups of water ready. Pour flour, milk and water mixture into the skillet. It will get thick quick, so add water until it is how you want it...

🌳

WDO: Ron may be almost as good selling insurance as his father, George, was—but probably not as good at cooking as Jane is. (Just kidding.)

YE OLDE YANKEE CLAMBAKE

Note to cook: act worried about whether or not food will be cooked—it adds to the fun.

Paul J. Smith, Vice President
Connecticut National Life
Hartford, CT

---

1 lobster (1¼ to 2 pounds) per person
1½ ears of corn per person
1 pound clams per person
3 bags seaweed (get through fish market)

Locate suitable back yard. Suitable may be defined as "any back yard that is suggested". Dig a pit about 5 feet by 4 feet and about 3 ½ to 4 feet deep. Line bottom and sides of pit completely with rocks. Fill pit with wood and burn as big and as hot a fire as possible for about 4 hours. Remove any sizeable pieces of wood that remain; spread hot ashes around pit.

Line bottom and sides of pit with wet seaweed. Put lobsters in burlap bags, place on bed of seaweed in pit and add light layer of seaweed. Put unhusked corn in burlap bag, place on layer of seaweed and add another light layer of seaweed. Put clams in burlap bag, place on layer of seaweed and cover with rest of seaweed. Cover pit with canvas, place dirt at edges of canvas to keep heat from escaping.

After about 3½ hours, open pit, remove and serve clams and reclose pit. After another ½ to 1 hour, remove corn and lobsters and serve. Total cooking time: 4 to 4½ hours.

❧

WDO: Assuming I could dig a pit that big in the lawn of the Governor's Mansion...would I have to get permission from the State Fire Marshal to build the requisite fire? Paul's recipe may not be worth much to those of us without ready access to seaweed, but if you can get him to tell you a joke, it's a keeper. He has managed to overcome his Northeastern roots to become a "normal" person in the eyes of those of us from the Midwest.

VEAL BY NEAL

Otherwise known to most of you as Veal Scallopini...
Neal E. Tyner, President, Ameritas
Lincoln, NE

½ cup Parmesan cheese, grated
1 tsp. salt
dash pepper
¼ cup flour
½ clove garlic
3 tbsp. olive oil
1 tbsp. lemon juice
½ cup dry white wine
½ cup consomme
1½ lbs. thinly sliced veal cutlets

Dry veal on paper towels. Mix flour, salt, pepper and cheese. Pound mixture into meat thoroughly.

Heat oil and garlic; brown meat on both sides. Remove garlic. Add lemon juice, wine and consomme; cover and simmer for 30 minutes. Serves 4.

WDO: Neal is a leader of the insurance industry in Nebraska, and has led his company through some very dramatic changes. When you are looking for a change from the regular menu, I suggest this entree might just fill the bill—if you can find the veal!

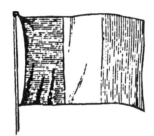

ITALIAN-O's

Those of us having one-syllabled last names beginning with "O" are understandably envious of those with many-syllabled last names ending in "O". There are two kinds of people in this world—Italians and those who wish they were Italians. Most of the men in this chapter THINK they are Italian. (There is a fellow in Monte Carlo by the name of Dario. When he walks into the room, women break out in a sweat. He IS Italian!)

ITALIAN BLUE CHEESE DRESSING

Cook's notes: this will help lower your blood pressure...it will also help prevent catching colds (no one will come near you)...also it is excellent without the cheese!
Vince Collura, Ass't General Manager
KFOR Radio, Lincoln, NE

½ of whole bulb of fresh garlic (medium size)
1½ tsp. sugar
1½ tsp. salt
1 tbsp. sweet basil, pulverized but not powdered
¾ cup wine vinegar
2¼ cup oil (½ olive and ½ Puritan)
3 oz. chunky blue cheese

Clean garlic pieces, put in blender. Add sugar, salt and ¼ cup wine vinegar. Mix thoroughly. Add the rest of the vinegar (½ cup) and the oil. Blend well. Add basil and blend again. Place in 1 qt. jar container. Add chunky blue cheese. Keep refrigerated. Stir well or shake before using.

WDO: Vince is justifiably proud of his Italian heritage. He learned to make Italian sausage from his father and continues the tradition. To be present while he is engaged in this activity is a treat in more ways than one.

PASTA POMMAROLA FISSO

"Fisso" means "fast," so if you're in the mood for Italian and you're in a hurry—this is the one to try.
Nicola Giussepe DiCicco, President/CEO
Midwestern National Life Insurance Co.
Mayfield Village, OH

---

2 32 oz. cans of whole, skinned tomatoes in tomato juice (imported from San Marzano, Italy if possible)
2 medium-sized onions
1/8 lb. butter (may be eliminated for those on cholesterol-free diets—use a little more oil)
1 small bunch of fresh basil—5 to 7 medium-sized leaves (if fresh not available, use ½ tsp. of dried leaves)
2-3 fresh cloves of garlic (medium size)
1 lb. of spaghettini—slightly more delicate version of spaghetti—(preferable brand is DeCecco, but any imported brand is good)
extra virgin olive oil
ground red pepper
salt
Locatelli cheese (a type of imported Romano cheese)

Break up the tomatoes into smaller pieces. This can be done by either chopping in ½ to 1 inch chunks, squeezing them by hand, mashing them with a potato masher or throwing them in the blender for a quick spin. Do not puree, but simply chop. Place entire contents into saucepan, add salt and ground red pepper to taste. Begin to simmer. We do not want a HOT sauce, just tasty.

Next, dice one of the two onions and place in a skillet which has already been prepared with 1/8 inch layer of olive oil. Brown the onions, but do not BURN them. Cook until olive oil and onions become thick. You may want to add a little salt to the mixture to encourage the thickening.

After the onions are carmelized, place the entire contents of the skillet into the simmering tomatoes. You may now add the other onion directly to the simmering tomatoes by rough-grating it into the pan. If you are unable to use the fresh basil and instead must use the dried basil, also add it to the mixture now. Otherwise wait until the time instructed below. Allow mixture to simmer for approximately ½ hour and

(continued)

prepare for the cooking of the spaghettini by placing a pot of water on the range to boil.

When the ½ hour has elapsed and the water has come to a boil, add a couple tablespoons of salt to the water and throw in your spaghettini, setting your timer for 6 minutes. Be sure to stir, especially while the spaghettini is still stiff, so that it doesn't stick. You now want to add your fresh basil by chopping it up, using scissors or otherwise, along with adding the garlic by using a garlic press and putting the entire contents into the sauce. You will note that both the basil and the garlic are put in the sauce at the very end since we want these flavors to be most prominent. Continue to simmer the sauce.

When the timer goes off, the spaghettini should be almost done. Please taste to be sure that you do not overcook. A good way to tell is to know when the pasta is "al dente" or "to the teeth." This means it is no longer crisp when chewed, but feels "substantial" rather than mushy.

Using a colander, remove the spaghettini from the water. Try to get as much water as possible out of the pasta. I always like to place a little sauce in the bottom of the platter before putting the pasta on to avoid sticking. As soon as the pasta is placed on the platter, pour some of the sauce on the pasta and mix well. This will prevent sticking together. Use only enough sauce to make the pasta reddish in color, so that the taste of the pasta itself comes through. Have extra sauce and the Locatelli cheese available at the table for individual preference.

❧

WDO: Nick is the "second most Italian man" I know. (If you think I'm going to tell you who the FIRST one is, you've got another think coming!) I've got a feeling you can make this dish in less time than it takes to read the recipe. This recipe has almost as many words at the U.S. Constitution!

ANTONIO'S RAVIOLI

Both of the following recipes, came from "Mama Raimondo" and are Italian treats at their finest.

Tony Raimondo, President/CEO
Behlen Manufacturing
Columbus, NE

4 cups sifted flour
½ tsp. salt
5 eggs
¼ cup lukewarm water

Sift flour onto a large board and make a well center. Add salt, eggs and water. Knead dough thoroughly about 1 minute until it is stiff and smooth. Add more flour if dough is too thin. Cover and set aside 10 minutes while filling is being prepared. Then divide dough into 3 parts, and roll each part out on a lightly floured board to paper thinness. Cut into 2 inch circles with cookie cutter or the top of a glass. Cut 2 rounds for each ravioli. Place a heaping tsp. of desired filling in the center of 1 circle, and cover with another circle. Press edges together with a fork to seal. Cook in 8 qts. boiling salted water until dough is tender. Serve with any tomato or meat sauce and sprinkle with grated cheese.

Note: Ravioli can be cut into 3 or 4 inch squares, if desired. Place 1 heaping tsp. filling in center of square and fold each square into a triangle. Seal edges with fork.

Filling:
1 lb. ricotta
2 eggs, well beaten
1 tbsp. grated Parmesan cheese
2 tbsp. minced parsley
½ tsp. cinnamon
1 tsp. sugar
salt and pepper

Mix all ingredients together until smooth. Use 1 heaping tsp. for each ravioli.

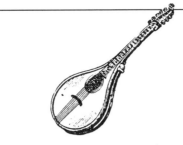

ANTONIO'S CANNOLI

Tony Raimondo, President/CEO
Behlen Manufacturing
Columbus, NE

1 cup flour
1 tbsp. sugar
pinch salt
1 tbsp. shortening
1 egg, slightly beaten
1 tsp. vanillla
1 tbsp. sugar
2 tsp. whiskey
2 tsp. water

Cut shortening into flour, add 1 tbsp. sugar and salt. Mix together egg, vanilla, 1 tbsp. sugar, whiskey and water. Mix liquid and flour mixtures. Knead well.

Dough should be stiff. If dough seems moist and sticky, add flour. If it is too dry, add more water. Cover dough and let stand 2 hours in a cool place. Then roll to paper thinness on lightly floured board. Cut into 5″ circles and wrap around a stick which is about 6 inches long and 1″ in diameter (or cannoli rod). Fold dough around stick loosely, so that ¼ inch of the stick protrudes at either end. Seal dough by brushing with egg yolk and fry 2 cannoli at a time in deep hot fat (4″ deep, 390⁰) for one minute or until brown on both sides. Lift out gently with a slotted spoon or tongs, drain on unglazed paper and cool. Remove sticks gently. If the cannoli are hot, hold them in the center with a cloth and push the stick out with a butter knife or the back of a spoon. Fill the cannoli with the following filling, using a butter knife, first from one end, then from the other. Dip the ends of the filling in tinted coconut or chopped nuts and sprinkle cannoli with confectioners sugar. Makes 18.

Note: the unfilled fried shells will keep for about 6 weeks in a cool, dry place. The uncooked dough will keep in the refrigerator for 2 or 3 days. Filled cannoli should be served immediately. Keep filling in the refrigerator unti you can serve cannoli and fill just before serving.

(continued)

Filling:
1 lb. ricotta cheese
1 tsp. vanilla
¾ cup powdered sugar
dash of cinnamon

Fold in:
½ cup Cool Whip
6 chopped maraschino cherries
¼ cup shaved milk chocolate
1 tsp. cherry juice (optional)

❧

WDO: Tony moved to Nebraska by choice and has been able to exert a positive influence on the further development of Behlen Manufacturing and the entire Columbus community. It's a delight to have him as a citizen of the state and a contributor to the cookbook.

ARDY'S LASAGNE

I made this 21 years ago for Christmas dinner and the family liked it so much that we have had it ever since for Thanksgiving AND Christmas!

Mrs. Joseph, (Ardy) Salerno
Omaha, NE

lasagne noodles
1 carton ricotta cheese
romano cheese
spaghetti sauce

Cook the noodles according to package directions. In a 9 x 13 pan layer:

noodles
sauce
ricotta (a dab every 2 inches)
sprinkle romano over all

Continue with noodles, sauce, ricotta and romano. Cover and bake in 350° oven for 30 minutes.

GREEN BEANS SICILIAN

This goes very nicely with lasagne...isn't that handy?

1 can green beans (cut or French)
2 cloves garlic, minced
3 tbsp. oil
2 tbsp. vinegar
salt and black pepper

Mix and chill before serving.

🌳

WDO: With a "simple" lasagne recipe and a sensational-sounding accompaniment, how could we have refused Ardy's offer of recipes for the cookbook?

AGLIO AND OLIO SUPREME

Pasta with a prosciutto flair...
Frank Santa-Donato, 2nd Vice President, LIMRA
Hartford, CT

⅓ cup olive oil
⅓ cup vegetable oil
3 lg. (5-6 sm.) garlic cloves, minced
½ lg. red or green pepper, diced
3 sm. scallions, diced
1 sm. plum tomato, diced
6 slices prosciutto, diced
sage
thyme
oregano
black pepper
parsley
grated cheese
½ lb. prepared pasta (fettucini)

Heat oil, saute garlic 2-3 minutes. Remove garlic and set aside. Saute pepper, scallions, tomato, and prosciutto for 3-5 minutes or until tender. Add spices to taste. Return garlic to pan. Saute 2-3 minutes more. Toss with pasta, add grated cheese to taste. Serves two.

VEAL PUMATE

Frank Santa-Donato, 2nd Vice President, LIMRA
Hartford, CT

veal cut or chop (for 2) seasoned
with salt, pepper and paprika
2 big cloves garlic
oil or margarine
1 tbsp. flour
¾ cup beef boullion
½ cup (or so) Marsala
juice of ½ lemon
sage
marjoram
several drops Muggi
several drops Kitchen Bouquet
cut up prosciutto
sun-dried tomatoes
parsley

Saute seasoned veal in oil or margarine and garlic. Remove meat and brown flour 2-3 minutes. Add boullion, wine, lemon juice and seasoning. Simmer sauce 2 minutes or so. Add prosciutto and dried tomatoes. Simmer 5 minutes more and serve over veal.

WDO: Frank is one of the many Italians who is "speechless" unless he is able to wave both hands at the same time. He was reluctant to send a recipe until I told him that Nick DiCicco was a contributor—this motivated him to take action in a matter of seconds.

OMELETTO
A LA TANTILLO

Bill prefers to call this an "Italian Hunt Breakfast"...and it's his book.

C.R. Tantillo, Agency Manager
Woodmen Accident and Life
Topeka, KS

1 medium potato
1 lg. sweet pepper (preferably red but green can be used)
1 lg. clove of garlic
1 med. onion
2 lg. or 4 med. mushrooms
7 eggs

Whip eggs thoroughly in a bowl and add approximately ¼ cup of water to mixture. Lightly whip in some salt and coarsely ground pepper.

Set up two frying pans; dice up the potato and put in one pan. Simmer on low heat until lightly brown. Cut pepper into small pieces and simmer in other pan until lightly brown.

Chop up onion and add to the frying pan with potatoes. Chop up mushrooms and add to frying pan with the peppers. Mix up each frying pan until ingredients are all slightly brown and then combine into a single large frying pan that has been basted with butter. Mix all ingredients together, add egg mixture and stir until eggs are almost done.

Place a cover on pan for a few more minutes and turn upside down onto a large platter. Add ground pepper and salt to taste. Serve hot with a generous glass of Chardonnay and a mixture of very cold fresh fruit.

❧

WDO: This feast defies description. One is never sure the recipe is the same twice. We have seen it prepared twice and on both occasions, the miracle was the lightning speed with which Chuck chopped up ingredients while not missing any commentary as to the Italian authenticity of the recipe.

CAESAR SALAD
A LA TANTILLO

Again, I defer to Bill, who says this one is the best he's ever tasted...a compliment hopefully deserved and graciously accepted.

Chuck Tantillo

---

1 lg. head romaine lettuce
4 lg. cloves garlic
1 can anchovies
1 cup olive oil
4 tbsp. wine vinegar or dry red wine (wine is preferred)
1 tbsp. Worcestershire sauce
Parmesan cheese
croutons (see below)

Start out with two large bowls, preferably an unfinished wooden bowl to mix the dressing in. Use the other bowl to break up the lettuce in small crisp squares of approximately 1-2 inches. Place bowl with lettuce in refrigerator to chill while preparing dressing.

For the best croutons, purchase a small loaf of brown and serve French bread. Break into finger size cubes and place in a shallow pan. Place under broiler, turning to brown on all sides.

Dressing:

1 large clove of garlic for each person. Crush into bottom of bowl and smash into as fine a number of pieces as possible. Take an entire tin of anchovies (minus four strips for later garnish) and empty into same bowl. Smash with back of fork until nothing is visible but very tiny pieces.

Add olive oil, vinegar or wine and squeeze in juice of ½ lemon (be careful no seeds fall in!). Add Worcestershire sauce and mix vigorously. Add some very coarsely ground black pepper and continue to beat until all ingredients are blended. Add croutons to bowl of lettuce. Add all of the dressing and toss until lettuce is coated evenly with the dressing. Generously sprinkle with Parmesan cheese, tossing until all lettuce is coated with the cheese.

Move into individual salad bowls, (preferably of a generous size), sprinkle additional Parmesan cheese and garnish with small strips of pimento and anchovy.

❧

WDO: Watching him prepare this is almost as much fun as eating it. As is the case with most good Italian cooks, Chuck does not spare the garlic—but he doesn't overdo it, either. He and Carol and Kay and I have had the best of times in our 25-year association...most (if not all) of them involving good food!

Frank Koehler and his grandaughter, Andrea, making Marzipan.

Gwen Hershberger bakes cookies with her grandchildren.

236

RELATIVELY
SPEAKING

It's amazing how many men and women, when asked for a recipe for the First Gentleman's Cookbook, responded they didn't cook "except...". In many instances this "except" was the recipe Mom used to fix, fondly recalled. What follows are some examples of these recipes. Others are found elsewhere in the book.

POLLY'S GOULASH

When I was growing up in Scottsbluff, we ate hamburger often, steak seldom. Mother used to throw together a concoction that she called goulash. We also called it "slumgullion" or "stuff", as in "please pass the stuff". I don't think there was ever a recipe and there isn't yet, but this is the way I remember it and about the way I make it.

Keith Blackledge, Editor
North Platte (NE) Telegraph

1 pound lean ground beef
1 large onion diced
2 or 3 stalks celery, sliced
2 cloves garlic, minced
2 or 3 carrots, sliced thin
1 green bell pepper, cut in strips
2 14½ oz. cans whole or stewed tomatoes
dried leaf oregano
dried leaf sweet basil
parsley flakes
1 cup shell macaroni

Crumble and brown beef in large frying pan. Remove from pan and set aside. Simmer onions in remaining fat until transparent, then pour off most of fat. Return ground beef to skillet with onions. Add celery, garlic, carrots, green pepper, tomatoes with juice and seasonings as desired. (I use plenty of oregano—a tablespoon or more.) We don't use it, but you could also add salt and pepper to taste.

Cover and let simmer on low heat until carrots and celery are crisp-tender (about half an hour). Meanwhile, cook macaroni according to directions on package. Drain. Add to skillet about 5 or 10 minutes before serving.

Almost anything leftover in the refrigerator, or on the shelf, or out of the garden can go in here. Corn is nice. Some grated cheddar or American cheese adds a different dimension. Zucchini goes well and probably should be added about halfway through the simmering since it cooks faster than carrots or celery. If it turns out too juicy you might want to add cornstarch (dissolved in cold water first) to thicken the sauce.

I quit adding ingredients when the skillet is full. This is quick, simple and I've never met anyone who didn't like it, whatever they called it!

❧

WDO: Many newspaper editors are noted for their ability to express themselves in writing. Few do a better job than Keith. Let's hope his recipes are as appetizing as his recitations.

SUSAN'S FAMOUS CHEESE SANDWICH

Your book is probably filled with exotic gourmet recipes that take some time to prepare. My entry, developed by my 11-year-old daughter for our family cookbook, is for those times when you are rushed and need a quick bite!
John Cochran, President
Norwest Bank
Omaha, NE

---

2 slices of bread
cheese in the bread

Microwave for one minute.

WDO: I think this recipe is notable for its simplicity and its selection by an obviously very loving father. Bravo.

240

GRANDMA CARVER'S PEANUT BUTTER CAKE

Five generations of our family have enjoyed or are enjoying this cake. One tip she gave me when I asked for the recipe was to buy a brand of peanut butter heavy on oil, to help make the cake moist. I have found a generic brand is good for this purpose. I also suggest using crunchy peanut butter instead of smooth for the frosting. This cake may not be recommended for calorie counters, but what the heck, all of us deserve a break once in awhile. If you like peanut butter, you'll absolutely love this.

Daryl M. Hall, Publisher
Kearney (NE) Hub

⅔ cup peanut butter
⅓ cup Crisco
1 cup sugar
2 eggs
1 cup milk
1½ cup sifted all-purpose flour
3 tsp. baking powder
1 tsp. salt
1 tsp. vanilla

Preheat oven to 350°. Grease and flour two 8″ layer pans.

Cream peanut butter, sugar and eggs; add milk. Sift flour, baking powder and salt together and add to mixture. Add vanilla, stir.

Bake approximately 30 minutes.

Cool and frost with a mixture of peanut butter, powdered sugar, vanilla and hot coffee.

If peanut butter is very oily, use 1 cup. Do not add more flour.

❧

WDO: It's a tossup between Keith Blackledge and Daryl Hall as to who writes the most convincing editorial. Since most of their editorials confirm my already held opinions, I have to declare it a draw.

SOUPY
CHOCOLATE CAKE

The Swiss are famous for their chocolate delicacies and this is no exception. The original recipe came from my Grandmother Kohler, a Swiss immigrant.

Jeanne James
Denton, NE

Cream:
½ cup shortening
1 cup white sugar
1 cup brown sugar
Add:
2 eggs
2 cups sifted cake flour
½ tsp. salt
½ cup sour milk
1 tsp. vanilla
2 squares melted unsweetened chocolate
Mix well and add:
1 cup boiling water with 1 tsp. baking soda in it

Bake at 375⁰...test for doneness after ½ hour.

KOENIGSBERG MARZIPAN

This is one of several German recipes my mother passed on to us. We use it at Christmas, with forms that are 30 to 60 years old and unfortunately are no longer manufactured. The result can be replicated by following the instructions in the recipe or molding it into miniature shapes of your choice.

Frank Koehler, City Manager
Scottsbluff, NE

1 lb. almonds
1 lb. powdered sugar
about ¼ cup warm water

Blanch and finely grind almonds. Knead the sugar with the almonds, adding some water a little at a time. The dough must be smooth and hold a dent if you press your finger in. Yield: about 22 pieces.

Let stand a day or more covered with a moist cloth. If the surface gets dry, knead it before you start working. This might help some if dough happened to get too soft. Use two or three symmetrical shapes...hearts, circles, etc. Roll out dough about ½ inch thick. Mark with the largest form, mark with the smaller form inside the first shape. Push out center portion. Then push out the "rim". Roll out a thin sheet of dough. Moisten the underside of the rim which you pushed out and press immediately on the thin sheet of dough cut with the larger same shape form. Set the piece on a board and tap slightly so rim and bottom stick together.

Broil on wood covered with glueless brown paper, like paper bags, to desired doneness. Watch constantly as it can burn easily. Fill with powdered sugar and lemon juice icing. Garnish with candied pineapple pieces.

❦

WDO: Frank, the longtime city manager of Scottsbluff, likes to perform this holiday ritual with his grandchildren. See photo on page 236.

GRANDMA'S CHOCOLATE CAKE

Here's a cake that is supposed to fall—believe it or not! Read on:
Otto Kotouc, Banker
Humboldt, NE

Separate 2 eggs.

Put whites in small bowl and beat until stiff, gradually adding ½ cup sugar.

In another bowl, beat 2 yolks with 2 whole eggs and ½ cup sugar until a lemon color.

Sift 2 rounded tbsp. flour and 2 rounded tbsp. cocoa, a pinch of salt, 1/8 tsp. cinnamon and 1/8 tsp. cloves and add slowly to the whole egg mixture.

Combine gently with egg white mixture. Put in greased pan and sprinkle sugar on top.

Bake in 350° oven for 30 minutes or until it falls. It is supposed to fall. Do not frost.

WDO: This one is so unusual, I have to try it soon. I've had cakes fall, but they weren't supposed to. I suppose this one won't collapse when it should. I'll be interested to see....

244

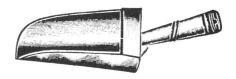

GRANDMA KROHN'S RAISIN BREAD

A long-awaited treat for Christmas and other occasions. Recipe makes 3 loaves, but she usually did 6 and many times 12. Friends, neighbors and others benefitted from her energy.
Bob Krohn, President/CEO, HDR, Inc.
Omaha, NE

1 cup water
1 package yeast
1 cup flour
1 tsp. sugar

Stir together in a medium bowl to make a "sponge". It should be rather thin, like pancake batter. Let it rise until at least double.

1½ cups milk
½ cup butter
¼ cup sugar
Put in saucepan and warm.
4 cups flour
1 tsp. salt

Put in large bowl, pour sponge over flour. Add milk mixture. Stir a bit and add 2 cups of raisins. Add a peeled cardamom seed if you want. (Remove several of the inner seeds, put in a towel and crush, then add to the flour mixture.)

After dough is mixed, scatter a bit of flour on top and knead until you are tired. Let rise to double. Form into loaves. Let rise to 1″ above pan. Bake at 350° for 50 minutes at Albion elevation. Let cool to 135° and eat with German meats and cheeses.

❧

WDO: The Krohn family is a fixture in the Albion area. While Bob and wife Myrna "strayed" to Omaha, he assures me that the recipe will work in other locations as well...and that people at vastly higher altitudes will know how to adjust for the desired results.

FRESH
CRANBERRY RELISH

A wonderful accompaniment for poultry, ham and pork. Keeps in refrigerator for a week or freezes well for later use.

Helen Long
Beemer, NE

---

1 package (12 oz.) fresh or frozen cranberries
1 large thin-skinned navel orange, unpeeled
1 large red delicious apple, unpeeled
¾ to 1 cup sugar

Wash the cranberries, orange and apple.

Slice unpeeled orange into eighths and remove seeds and white membrane. Core the unpeeled apple and slice into eighths.

Place half the cranberries, half the orange slices and half the apple slices in food processor container. Process until mixture is evenly chopped. Transfer to bowl. Repeat with remaining cranberries, orange and apple.

Stir in sugar to desired sweetness. Store in covered glass jar in refrigerator at least 3 hours to ripen.

WDO: In case you're wondering why this one is in the "Relatively Speaking" category...it's because Helen Long is Julie Seever's "mom". In case you're wondering who Julie Seever is, see page 324.

DAD'S OYSTER DRESSING

Submitted in memory of my father, Dr. Porter F. Dodson, who was born and raised in Wilbur, NE. This has been a Thanksgiving tradition in the Dodson and Neal households for generations.

Kathleen M. Neal, Wife of Vice President/Marketing
Woodmen Accident and Life
Lincoln, NE

---

3 loaves white bread several days old—broken up

or

2 loaves bread and 1 package
Pepperidge Farm dressing mix
10 large onions
1 pound oleo
2 pints fresh oysters
2 tsp. salt
½ tsp. pepper
1 tsp. poultry seasoning

Thanksgiving Eve, slice onions and simmer in oleo 3-4 hours. Simmer turkey neck, liver, gizzard and heart 3-4 hours. Break up bread, allow to dry.

Thanksgiving morning, warm giblets and onions. Cut up giblets and oysters. Mix all with seasonings and bread. Use oyster liquor and giblet broth to moisten.

Recipe provides several baking pans of dressing in addition to turkey stuffing.

CHOCOLATE PIE

It was over 100 years ago that my mother went west with her family to homestead land in the Dakota Territory. As a little girl, she learned how to cook and bake, which she continued to do all of her life. One of the most appetizing recipes she left to her children is this one.

Vance Rogers, Former President
Nebraska Wesleyan University
Lincoln, NE

2 cups of sugar
4 heaping tbsp. of cocoa
4 heaping tbsp. of flour

Mix these ingredients together, adding small amounts of water to make a smooth paste. Separate 4 eggs, saving the whites for meringue.

Beat the yolks; add 2 tbsp. of melted butter, 2 cups of milk and egg yolks to the first mixture. Cook over SLOW fire until thick and starts to bubble. After removing from fire, add 2 tsp. vanilla. Pour into baked pie shell and add meringue.

WDO: Vance will long be remembered for having made Nebraska Wesleyan a leading educational institution not only in Nebraska, but in the United States. One is never disappointed when Vance is asked to come to the microphone to speak. I wonder if he'd be interested in going on a promotional tour for the cookbook?

WORLD WAR II MARTINI

This recipe was handed down from an uncle who served in the Army Air Corps in World War II. He vouched that he had done a thorough search and testing for the perfect martini on three continents and many islands in the company of only the most discriminating companions. The only alternative in the procedure, he recommended, was to put the shaken mixture outdoors for five minutes, instead of the freezer, when socializing in Thule, Greenland in January.

Tom White, Editor
Lincoln (NE) Star

---

3 parts Beefeaters Gin
1 part vodka
⅓ part vermouth
3 drops scotch
1 drop aromatic bitters

Pour ingredients into shaker over several ice cubes. Carefully shake to clink the ice, but not so vehemently as to bruise the gin. Chill in freezer for 15 minutes. When chilled, serve immediately in long-stemmed martini glasses over olive or lemon peel.

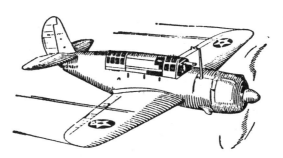

Roger Wehrbein knows where "the beef" is.

Dan Lynch...you're not seeing spots; that's his apron.

Sen. Bernice Labedz' Family (she's the 3rd from youngest).

250

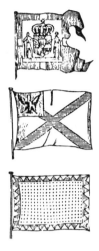

ETHNIC EPICURES

Nebraska would not be Nebraska without its rich ethnic heritage. Influences from virtually every European nation and most Asian and Spanish-speaking countries continue to benefit our state and make it unique. One "bonus" is the treasure of ethnic foods, a few of which are presented here.

TAMALE PIE

I learned to like this recipe while attending junior high in San Diego in the early 30's. It was served twice a week for lunch— you ate it or went hungry!

George Abel, President
NEBCO, Lincoln, NE

Saute in lightly greased skillet:

1 pound ground chuck
1 chopped onion

When the meat is well browned and the onion translucent (drain off excess grease), add:

8 oz. can of Hunt's tomato sauce
½ tsp. garlic powder
1 cup water
¼ tsp. pepper
½ tsp. salt
2 tsp. chili powder
1 cup drained whole kernel corn
⅓ cup chopped green pepper
(seeds and membrane removed)
4 oz. can chopped or sliced ripe olives

Simmer 15 minutes. Preheat oven to 425°.

Meanwhile, sift and mix together:

¾ cup yellow cornmeal
1 tbsp. flour
1 tbsp. sugar
½ tsp. salt
1½ tsp. double-acting baking powder

Moisten with:

1 beaten egg
⅓ cup milk

Mix lightly and stir in:

1 tbsp. vegetable oil

Place meat mixture in a greased 2-quart casserole and cover evenly with the cornbread topping. The topping will sink into the meat mixture, but will rise during baking and form a layer of cornbread. Bake about 20 minutes or until cornbread is brown.

Optional: garnish finished product with shredded cheddar cheese and/or sour cream.

CONCHITA'S PAELLA

A "special occasion" meal that is as good as it looks.
Conchita Alonso
Lincoln, NE

2 cups rice
½ cup olive oil
3 chicken breasts
(skinned, boned and cut
into pieces)
½ pound cubed ham
½ cup chopped onion
1 tsp. minced garlic
1 large bay leaf
1 chopped green pepper
8 oz. can tomato sauce
1 tsp. salt
¼ tsp. pepper
1½ lbs. fresh shrimp
(shelled and deveined)

12-14 clams in shell
(scrubbed)
3 lobster tails cut
into rings
1 lb. crab meat or scallops
1 lb. red snapper cut into
pieces
1½ qts. chicken broth
12 oz. beer
1 cup sherry
1 cup frozen peas
few shreds saffron or
1 tbsp. paprika
7 oz. can pimentos

Heat oil in paella pan. Cook chicken for about 10 minutes, turning until light brown on all sides. Add onion and garlic and cook for 2 minutes. Add tomato sauce, salt, pepper, ham and seafood and cook for 5 minutes or until clam shells are barely open. Remove clams and save for garnish.

Add rice, fish, water, green pepper, beer, sherry, saffron or paprika, bay leaf, broth and peas. Mix well, bring to a boil, then cover and cook on low heat for 25 minutes or until rice is tender. Garnish with pimentos and clams. Serves 12-14.

WDO: Conchita is as well known for her good taste in food (and the ability to prepare it) as she is for her good taste in clothing (and the ability to sell it).

ORIENTAL SALAD

This spinach dish came from Charlyne's mother. Even people who don't like spinach like it fixed this way.
Dennis and Charlyne Berens
Editor/Publisher, Seward (NE) County Independent

2 lbs. spinach, washed
2 cans water chestnuts, sliced
½ lb. bacon, fried crisp
4 hard boiled eggs, chopped

Toss together. When ready to serve, add dressing and toss again. Serves 10-12.

DRESSING

1 cup salad oil
1 tbsp. Worcestershire sauce
¾ cup sugar
1 medium onion, chopped
⅓ cup catsup
2 tsp. salt
¼ cup vinegar

Put all ingredients in blender and process until smooth.

CANTONESE TOMATO CHICKEN WINGS

This can be served in a crockpot to keep warm-m-m-m-
Bruce Buehler, M.D., Director
Meyer Childrens Rehabilitation Institute
University of Nebraska Medical Center, Omaha, NE

2 lb. chicken wings
1 tbsp. grated ginger
4 cloves pressed garlic
4 tbsp. peanut oil
2 cups chopped tomatoes
3 tbsp. hoisin sauce
3 tbsp. soy sauce
2 tbsp. red wine vinegar
2 tsp. sugar
1 tbsp. cornstarch in 2 tbsp. cold water

Remove wing tips with a cleaver. Heat peanut oil in a wok, add the ginger and garlic. Heat 1-2 minutes, then add the wings and stir-fry until braised.

Combine the rest of the ingredients (except the cornstarch) in a pot. Add the wings and simmer for 25 minutes. When the meat easily pulls off the wings, remove to a platter. Bring the liquid to a boil, add the cornstarch and thicken. Pour over the wings and serve.

OYSTER SAUCE MUSHROOMS

NOTE: This does not taste like oysters.
Bruce Buehler, M.D., Director
Meyer Childrens Rehabilitation Institute
University of Nebraska Medical Center, Omaha, NE

---

24 mushrooms, brushed and the end of stem removed
4 tbsp. cold water
3 tbsp. cornstarch
1½ cup beef stock (canned or boullion cubes)
4 tbsp. oyster sauce
1 tbsp. rice wine

Bring the beef stock to a boil, add the mushrooms. Turn down to a simmer. Cook covered for 20-25 minutes. Remove the mushrooms to a serving dish. Keep warm.

Return the beef stock to a boil, add the oyster sauce and the rice wine. Stir well and add the cornstarch mixture. Boil until thickened. Pour over the mushrooms and serve.

WDO: Bruce spent his military years in the Orient. Most physicians and/or soldiers spent their time in bistros—Bruce spent his time studying cooking with Oriental families. The result is that he can host a nine-course meal unlike any other Occidental in the State of Nebraska.

OLD WORLD BLACK BREAD

My brother, a bachelor, said this was the "perfect" bread—a slice or two at breakfast provided cocoa and coffee—and it was tops for pre-dinner cocktails when spread with cheese, etc. He was the only Raglin boy to enter Mom's kitchen other than to 1) eat, or 2) empty the garbage.

Jim Raglin, General Manager, Nebraska Press Ass'n
Lincoln, NE

3¾ cups rye flour
3¼ cups all purpose flour
2 packages dry yeast
½ cup warm water

"A"

½ cup unsweetened cocoa (that's right, cocoa)
¼ cup sugar
2 tbsp. caraway seeds
2 tsp. salt
2 tsp. instant coffee crystals (that's right, coffee)

"B"

2 cups water
¼ cup vinegar
¼ cup dark corn syrup
¼ cup margarine or butter

Mix the rye and white flour in a large bowl. Reserve 3 cups of this mixture.

Sprinkle yeast over warm water; stir until dissolved. In a large bowl, stir together reserved 3 cups flour and group "A" above. In a medium saucepan combine "B" above. Heat over low heat until just warm. (Butter doesn't have to melt.) Add "B" to "A" and blend well. Stir in rest of flour, 1 cup at a time, until dough doesn't cling to side of bowl. Let it (and you) rest 10 minutes. Knead dough until smooth and elastic (about 15 minutes). Put it in greased bowl; turn greased side up. Cover. Let rise in warm place about 1 hour or until double. Make into loaves. Put into greased bread pans. Let rise again and bake at 375° for 40 minutes or until done.

❧

WDO: Jim has the reputation of becoming a "lightning rod". He once wrote an article critical of those who grew and prepared zucchini. Some 12 years later, he continues to be known as "Count Zucchini" and receives mail lambasting him for his cynical view of the great (?) vegetable.

POLISH BORSCHT

For a lower calorie version, you can eliminate the eggs and cream and halve the amount of sausage.
Ray Starostka, Agroservice Inc.
Silver Creek, NE

2 eggs, beaten
⅔ cup water
2 tbsp. flour
1 qt. buttermilk
1 tsp. salt
2 tbsp. vinegar
½ cup cream
2 hard boiled eggs, peeled
2 cloves garlic, chopped
1 small ring Polish sausage, cut into ¼″ slices

Mix beaten eggs and water. Blend in flour. Add to buttermilk in a 2 qt. saucepan and blend. Over medium heat, bring mixture to a slow boil, stirring constantly (about 5 minutes). Add salt, vinegar and cream. Stir in chopped boiled eggs, garlic and sausage. Let simmer 5 minutes more.

May be served hot over broken pieces of toast or fried potatoes. Also may be chilled and served cold.

WDO: Shows you what I know...I always thought borscht had cabbage in it. Oh well, I'm not going to argue over a Polish recipe with a man named Starostka.

SUKIAKI

The following combination of foods comes as close to what I remember as being Sukiaki from my days in Hawaii. It is a relatively easy dish to make and one that allows preparation prior to guests arriving. The actual cooking takes place when you are ready to eat. My first recollection of eating this is 1964 while visiting a family who lived in Papakolea, which is an Hawaiian homestead area near Punchbowl Cemetery on Oahu. I can still remember the pungent odors and such a wonderful taste. I have tried to recreate both, but I've come to believe that one must have the Pacific Ocean and the flowers of Hawaii to make it complete.

Brent R. Stevenson, Vice Chancellor
University of Nebraska Medical Center
Omaha, NE

1 lb. of beef sliced for sukiaki (if the butcher is puzzled, ask him to do it as if he were doing it for French Dip, then cut the slices in quarters)
3 medium sized onions, chopped into chunks
1 lb. sliced carrots
1 can whole water chestnuts
1 can bean sprouts or ½ lb. fresh bean sprouts
1 sm. head cabbage, cut and chopped into 2″ pieces

Cooking sauce:
1 cup soy sauce
¾ cup water or white cooking wine
4 cloves garlic and 4 equal amounts of fresh ginger
brown sugar to desired level of sweetness

Prepare sauce in wok or large, deep frying pan. Add liquid ingredients and press garlic and ginger through a garlic press. Discard fiber. Add sugar and bring to low heat. Sauce should have a light, sweet taste.

Bring liquid mixture to a boil and add beef. When beef begins to turn from red to pink, add carrots and onions. You want the vegetables to be crisp, but well steamed. Therefore, just wait a few minutes and add the remaining ingredients. Lightly stir enough to mix ingredients. When beef is a pinkish brown, the dish should be ready. Serve with steamed rice.

(continued)

The amounts above are for 2-3 people. The recipe can be increased and made for 8-10 people. Generally, this is about as much as a full-sized wok will hold. Because it cooks so fast, we have prepared this for more and always have a second batch ready to throw in after the first has been served. If not used the same night, it is a tremendous leftover. Bon appetit!

❧

WDO: Brent's culinary skills are second to none. If you receive an invitation from Brent and Vickie, by all means you should cancel everything and attend. His ability to produce a masterpiece in the kitchen is something to behold.

SPARERIBS AND SAUERKRAUT

You don't have to be German to enjoy these, but it helps.
Willis Strauss, Retired Chairman, Enron
Omaha, NE

Parboil ribs (in serving size pieces) until tender...in water with salt, pepper, bay leaf and onions added.

In casserole, put drained kraut; top with lemon juice, slices of onion and lemon.

Top with ribs and some broth from the parboiling. Cover and bake slowly until ribs are very tender.

ECHRICH

Translates to smoked or Polish sausage, tasty in any tongue!
Patrick Thomas
Chicago, IL

cut sausage into ½ inch slices

cook in open fry pan on low to medium heat with:

2 tbsp. stone ground mustard
2 tbsp. honey
1 cup dry white wine

Simmer until all fluids are absorbed.

WDO: I can't decide whether to serve this for breakfast, an appetizer, a snack or a side dish with a meal! (may have to investigate each alternative...)

Harold Andersen—"cheers"—
what's that paper he's reading?

J. Alan Cramer and friend

MEDIA MEN AND WOMEN

Nebraska is blessed with both print and electronic media of high quality. Living in the news spotlight, one pays particular attention to the complimentary and critical comments from the media. With few exceptions, the Governor has been treated fairly by Nebraska media.

POTATO SALAD

Seasonings and vinegar go directly on the potatoes so the spicy,
sweet and sour flavors will be absorbed.

Marc Anthony, Editor
Scottsbluff Star Herald, Scottsbluff, NE

2½ cups cooked sliced potatoes
1¼ tsp. salt
1 tsp. sugar
2 tsp. vinegar

Toss the above, then add:

½ cup chopped onion
½ cup sliced celery
¼ cup sweet pickle relish with mustard seed
¾ cup salad dressing
(Miracle Whip light may be substituted)

Toss to mix and fold in 2 hard cooked eggs, chopped. Chill and serve.

SCHAUM TORTE

When we were students at the University of Missouri years ago, our landlady, Allie Clayton, who was the wife of the Presbyterian minister to students, made this for special occasions.
Keith Blackledge, Editor
North Platte (NE) Telegraph

6 egg whites
2 cups granulated sugar
1 tsp. vanilla
1 tsp. vinegar
2 pints fresh or frozen strawberries or other fruit
½ pint whipping cream

Beat the egg whites at room temperature to a stiff, dry froth. Add sugar a little at a time. Add vanilla and vinegar. Grease a springform pan and pour in ⅔ of the mixture. Make small kisses dropped from a teaspoon with the rest of the mixture and place on a greased tin. Bake 60 minutes in a very slow oven, 225°.

Cool torte and cover with fruit, then whipped cream. Decorate top with baked kisses. The torte can be made the day before you want to serve it and assembled at the last minute.

❧

WDO: This one was submitted by husband Keith Blackledge, who wonders why his wife hasn't made him any Schaum Torte for about 20 years? No special occasions? (No further comments from here!)

WILD GOOSE

It's simple...it's delicious...everything can be done in advance!
J. Alan Cramer, Publishing
Member-Game and Parks Comm.
Wayne, NE

Place goose on rack in open roaster. Open two cans of clear consomme; pour over goose. Pour two cans of water into roaster. Take can of sherry, pour over bird. Salt and pepper goose well; then turn breast side down on rack. Bake at 350° for 2½ hours or until goose is tender—basting every 15 minutes. If you are very busy and cannot baste that often, cover pan. (Open method is preferred). When goose is done, slice off and return meat to broth. Keep warm until ready to serve.

WDO: Alan and I attended the Republican National Convention in Miami in 1972. There we set a record for attending the least number of business sessions, but acquiring the most suntan of any delegates, alternates or guests.

COMPANY
PORK CHOPS

This recipe was a favorite when I was in college. It's simple but it tastes great.

Dave Dawson, Managing Editor
Columbus (NE) Telegram

---

4 to 6 pork chops
1 can cream of mushroom soup
½ can red wine
salt and pepper to taste

Brown pork chops in large skillet (about 10-15 minutes). Combine mushroom soup and wine, pour over chops. Reduce heat and simmer for 1-1½ hours, turning chops and stirring as necessary.

The soup mixed with the wine will make the sauce appear purple when first poured over chops. But as the sauce cooks, it turns into a wonderful brown gravy that is great over mashed potatoes.

CRAB APPETIZER

Here's a favorite that even I can put together! A definite man-pleaser.

Don Gill, Director/Development
Nebraska ETV
Lincoln, NE

2 8-oz. packages of cream cheese (soft)
roll into log shape and chill—

Mix:
1 can crabmeat
¾ cup catsup
¼ cup Savory sauce
½-1 tsp. onion juice
¼-½ tsp. lemon juice

Chill.

Pour over cream cheese log before serving with club crackers.

WDO: Don has been a radio and TV personality for many years. While he has been a "public figure", I think this may be the first time he's "gone public" with his culinary skills.

HAPPY MARRIAGE

This recipe is guaranteed to work—it's simple and foolproof.
John Gottschalk, President/CEO
Omaha (NE) World-Herald

To keep your marriage brimming with love in the loving cup, when you're wrong, admit it—and when you're right, shut up.

❧

WDO: How can I elaborate on such words of wisdom...right, Carmen?

PANHANDLE FIESTA BEANS

Daryl M. Hall, Publisher
Kearney (NE) Hub

The key to success in preparing beans is to always select the best. There are no beans better that those grown in the great Panhandle of Nebraska! Flavoring for this recipe has evolved through the years, according to changing tastes and my aging digestive tract. It is a great dish to prepare and freeze for later use and it is an excellent meal on cold winter days.

1 lb. Nebraska Panhandle Pinto Beans
1 large ham hock
1 chopped medium-sized onion
1 tbsp. chili powder (or to taste)
1 tsp. cumin
3 16 oz. cans stewed tomatoes

Wash and sort beans; soak overnight. Place beans and soak water in crockpot. Add cut up ham hock and chopped onion. Cook on high temperature for 2 hours. Lower temperature and continue cooking for 4-5 hours, or until ham hock is cooked and easily cut.

Cut away all fat, rind and bone and discard. Cut meat into small pieces and return to pot.

Carefully remove excess broth from crockpot to allow room for addition of stewed tomatoes. Add chili powder and cumin (these can be put in when cooking is first started if you prefer) and stir well.

Cook for 2-3 more hours on low, or until beans are well done. Frequent stirring and tasting is recommended so that additional chili powder can be added, according to taste. Addition of salt to beans is not normally needed due to the salt content in the ham hocks, however, it can be added according to taste.

❦

WDO: see my comments on page 241.

SPECIAL MEATBALLS

First of all, be advised that this recipe makes about 70 meat-balls, which may sound like a lot, but keep in mind they freeze very nicely!

Scott Young & Cathy Blythe
KFOR Radio Show Personalities
Lincoln, NE

---

3 lb. ground ham
2 lb. ground pork
2 lb. ground beef (low fat, high quality)
3 eggs
3 cups crushed graham crackers
2 cups milk

Squish together in a big bowl or pan. (Note: if you call a couple of days ahead to your favorite meat counter at your favorite store, you can get them to grind up the meat and mix it together for you.)

Meatballs are best if frozen first...they retain their shape better when you bake them. Put on cookie sheet and freeze, then bag the ones you're not using now and bake the rest for 1 hour at 350°.

Pour following sauce over them and bake for another hour:

---

2 cans tomato soup
¾ cup vinegar
2¼ cups brown sugar
2 tbsp. dry mustard

WDO: These two radio personalities have developed quite a reputation in the Lincoln area. They have also produced a cookbook annually for the past several years. It's only fair that they have their recipe in my book inasmuch as my recipes have appeared in theirs.

CHEESE FRENCHEES

In earlier years, every big town in Nebraska had a KING'S FOOD HOST, famous for its telephone in each booth and "frenchee" sandwiches. With the unfortunate demise of this restaurant chain, we who were hooked on these sandwiches have been known to travel great distances and go to great lengths for the famous dish. In fact, this recipe was lifted from the OMAHA WORLD HERALD.

Nick Partsch, General Manager
Nebraska City (NE) News-Press

---

6 slices of sandwich bread
6 slices of American cheese
mayonnaise type salad dressing
1 well beaten egg
½ cup milk
¾ cup flour
½ tsp. salt
finely crushed corn flakes or corn flake crumbs
your favorite oil for deep frying

Make three sandwiches using mayonnaise according to your taste.

Cut off crusts, cut sandwiches diagonally into quarters.

Beat together egg, milk, flour and salt. Dip sandwich triangles into batter and roll in crushed corn flakes.

Freezing sandwiches before frying helps them hold together better. Fry at 375° until golden.

WDO: Nick tells me that the Embers Restaurant in Nebraska City serves these as an appetizer. I know there are a lot of people out there who are glad to have that information as well as this recipe.

GOOSE BLIND PORRIDGE

Don't tell anyone what's in this soup, as even people who HATE sauerkraut love it. It is especially satisfying, warming and comforting after a cold morning in a goose blind.

Jack Pollack, Publisher
Keith County News
Ogallala, NE

---

6 strips of bacon
1 lb. polish sausage, sliced
1 small onion, chopped
2 tbsp. tomato paste
3 cans (10½ oz.) beef broth
3 soup cans water
½ cup pearl barley
1 can (16 oz.) sauerkraut, drained well
1½ tsp. paprika

In skillet, fry bacon until crisp. Drain on paper towels and crumble. Brown chopped onion lightly in bacon grease. Drain with bacon and discard grease from skillet. In same skillet, brown Polish sausage slices lightly to remove excess fat. Drain. Place meats and onion in soup kettle. Add all other ingredients EXCEPT sauerkraut and paprika. Bring to boil, cover, lower heat and simmer 30 minutes. Add sauerkraut and paprika; stir and simmer 25 minutes longer, covered.

Serves 6.

❧

WDO: I wish I would have had this recipe before hunting season last fall...I may not wait till next fall to try it, however.

HASH BROWN POTATOES

Idaho potatoes will work, but Nebraska's are best. Using anything but a fresh potato is cheating. The careful cook will make sure no potato juice drips from the kitchen counter into the silverware drawer.

Emil Reutzel, Editor
Norfolk (NE) Daily News

You need about half as many good size potatoes as there are people to serve, especially since dainty eaters may only want half of one portion. A bit of diced onion is good, but not essential. Grate the potatoes, taking care not to slice thumb and finger tips by thinking it possible to avoid ALL waste.

Heat a frying pan, preferably cast iron, to the point where butter does not burn and keep it at low temperature for cooking the potatoes (grated) which you have formed into a patty. Salt and pepper can be added during the cooking process. It is important to keep the pan buttered and to put a little butter on the top before the patty is turned. Cook and turn until crisp on both sides. As for time, it takes about as long as a tall Bloody Mary lasts for a moderate drinker.

WDO: Emil has seen the city of Norfolk during good times and bad. Fortunately, he is able to put Norfolk on the map no matter how things are going economically and is as much a positive influence on that area of the state as anyone.

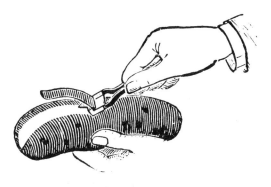

MARY'S COFFEE CAKE

This recipe "from a newspaper friend" is moist, has an unusual texture and keeps well.

Mrs. Kenton R. (Mary) Thomas
Wife of Publisher, Beatrice (NE) Sun

1½ cups butter
3 cups sugar
3 eggs
1½ tsp. baking powder
12 oz. sour cream
¾ tsp. vanilla
3 cups sifted cake flour
½ tsp. salt

Topping:
3 rounded tbsp. brown sugar
½ cup English walnuts, chopped
1½ tsp. cinnamon

Cream butter (can use ½ margarine) and sugar well with mixer. Add the eggs and vanilla and beat or cream. Stop using mixer.

Carefully add sifted dry ingredients, alternating with sour cream, handling as little as possible. Put half of batter in well greased bundt or angel food cake pan — sprinkle topping over and cover with rest of batter.

Bake at 350⁰ for 1 hour and 15 minutes (time may vary) or until it tests done. Cool before taking from pan. Let coffee cake ripen or mellow by keeping it covered with foil for 1 day. Sprinkle with powdered sugar before serving.

❧

WDO: Sounds like another good company or Christmas morning dish. Nice to get all of the cooking and cleaning up done ahead of time.

THE BEST THING YOU CAN DO TO A CARROT SOUP

Historical note: I tried a more basic recipe on a cold November Saturday about five years ago. Mary was pleased that I had cooked dinner, surprised that I tried something new, and shocked to find that it was very tasty. We have since added a few ingredients and tried it both hot and cold. It's good both ways. I think it is best after the leftover portion has been in the refrigerator a day and is heated up again. But then, editors' tastes have always been suspect.

Tom White, Editor
Lincoln (NE) Star

1 lb. carrots	½ tsp. sugar
½ lb. potatoes	1 cup heavy cream
2 tbsp. butter	½ tbsp. Worcestershire
¾ cup chopped onion	sauce
6 cups chicken broth	1 cup cream
½ tsp. thyme	salt and pepper to taste
½ tsp. Tabasco sauce	sprinkling of dill

Peel carrots and slice. Peel potatoes and cube. In a large saucepan, saute onions in butter until transparent. Add the carrots, potatoes and broth and bring to boil. Add thyme and then simmer for about 30 minutes until the carrots are tender. Using a strainer or spoon, separate the vegetables from the broth. Put the vegetables in a food processor (or blender) and puree until smooth.

Return vegetable mixture to broth. Whisk until blended. Heat briefly. Stir in remaining ingredients except for dill.

If serving hot, bring to near boil. If serving cold, chill thoroughly. Sprinkle with dill before serving.

❧

WDO: Tom is a prolific writer. Until he submitted his recipe for the World War II martini, I was unable to understand the source of some of his editorial inspiration. Now it becomes clear! (See page 249.)

Bill Smith gets ready to chop, chop, the celery, celery.

Jerry Mapes...yipes, stripes.

Dale Jensen—a loaf of bread, a glass of wine, and WOW!

STUCK ON PEANUT BUTTER

At the Saturday morning breakfast roundtable I usually attend, the cookbook has been an occasional topic of conversation, with "courteous" interest being expressed by those present. That is, until the subject of peanut butter sandwiches came up. An entire hour of controversy raged on the first occurrence...and that was only the beginning. I never realized something so simple could be such a sticky subject. Following are a few of the opinions contributed on this issue.

"CECH"-OSLOVAKIAN PEANUT BUTTER SANDWICH RECIPE

1. Single face sandwich:
   one slice bread
   generous helping of peanut butter spread evenly
   on one side
2. Double face sandwich:
   two slices bread
   generous helping of peanut butter spread evenly
   on both slices
3. Peanut butter and jelly sandwich:
   one slice of bread
   generous helping of peanut butter spread evenly
   on one half
   generous helping of jelly spread evenly on opposite half
4. Peanut butter and pickle sandwich
   one slice of bread
   generous helping of peanut butter spread evenly
   on one half
   one whole dill pickle (no need to slice) on opposite half
5. Peanut butter and banana sandwich
   one slice of bread
   generous helping of peanut butter spread evenly
   on one half
   one whole banana (no need to slice) on opposite
   half

For toasted peanut butter sandwiches, place any of above
in toaster for surprising results.

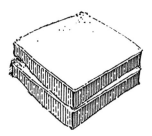

APPLE'S PEANUT BUTTER TREATISE

Since you asked...below are listed a few footnotes for your peanut butter sandwich section.

Robert Norris, Owner, Nebraska Neon
Lincoln, NE

First, it should be clearly understood that it is only necessary to enumerate these items for the nouveau peanut butterian (but-TER-yan, accent on the second syllable), as the true connoisseur knows and appreciates fully the finer points of the preparation and consumption of peanut butter.

1. Always start with creamy—this allows more flexibility when building the sandwich.

2. The very freshest bread is a must. (Personally, wheat is preferred.)

3. Never...never, ever...defile a peanut butter sandwich by including mayonnaise. This sacrilege is practiced by a few of the unclean who pass themselves off as true peanut butterians, but it changes the taste completely and must not be allowed.

4. A little-known fact is that the grilled peanut butter sandwich has surpassed the grilled cheese as a partner for tomato soup on a cold winter day. (And put a little fried bacon in the grilled P.B. to make it a runaway hit.)

5. A few popular P.B. partners between the slices:
    -sprouts and chopped pecans
    -thin sliced cucumber
    -sliced sweet pickle

6. Finally—True peanut butterians always "main line" a glob just before putting the jar away. The most common method is using the knife previously used to spread the P.B. (this hides the telltale track one's finger leaves in the jar when you have no utensil and have to "go bare").

Hope this has been helpful...

❧

WDO: Bob's nickname is "Apple". At our every Saturday breakfast, I casually mentioned receiving a recipe for making a peanut butter sandwich. I thought that would be the end of it until I heard Apple's objections. They came forth in gushes of emotional outburst. Thus we opened what is now called a "sticky issue".

ORR'S PEANUT BUTTER SANDWICH CHECKLIST

Choose no more than two from each category:

PEANUT BUTTER
- ☐ creamy
- ☐ crunchy
- ☐ super-chunky
- ☐ natural
- ☐ unnatural

BREAD
- ☐ white
- ☐ whole wheat
- ☐ rye (light, dark, seeded, unseeded)
- ☐ pumpernickel
- ☐ sourdough
- ☐ raisin
- ☐ oatmeal
- ☐ multigrain
- ☐ homemade
- ☐ unhomemade

ADDED FEATURES
- ☐ mayonnaise
- ☐ salad dressing
- ☐ jelly (flavor of choice)
- ☐ pickles (sweet, dill, bread 'n butter)
- ☐ taco sauce
- ☐ salsa
- ☐ potato chips
- ☐ corn chips
- ☐ Cool Whip (really!)
- ☐ syrup
- ☐ sugar
- ☐ popcorn
- ☐ bacon
- ☐ raisins
- ☐ cheese (choice of kinds)
- ☐ onion
- ☐ olives (green or ripe—stuffed or unstuffed)
- ☐ salted
- ☐ unsalted

OPTIONS
- ☐ toasted
- ☐ untoasted

PEANUT BUTTER POWER BREAKFAST

Okay, okay. Why else would I get involved in this sticky issue of Bill's except to fill what would otherwise have been a blank page at the end of this section? To prevent such a waste of space, I hereby divulge my heretofore confidential "P.B." (as Bob Norris puts it) creation. It's a fast, easy energy-packed and delicious way to start the day.

Pam Eiche, Editor
First Gentleman's Cookbook

---

1) Toast two slices Pepperidge Farm Cinnamon Raisin Bread;

2) Spread one slice with creamy peanut butter; spread other slice with honey;

3) Slap sticky sides together and consume with milk, coffee or orange juice.

RESTAURANT PROS' PROSE

New Orleans has its "underground gourmet guide" to fine restaurants...but then their water is all above ground. Since Nebraska has a wealth of underground water, we hereby present this "above-ground guide" to some of our fine restaurants. I should also mention that nearly 100 letters requesting recipes were sent to restaurants throughout the state. Not as many replied as we anticipated...guess that means a lot of Nebraska chefs who cook for a living want to keep their jobs secure and their recipes secret.

C. Floridia of La Strada 72 fame...look at those deserts!

MOM'S CHILI

Paul Stec, Big J's Family Restaurant
Broken Bow, NE

7 lbs. hamburger
1 green pepper, chopped
1 small onion, chopped
3 stalks celery, chopped
1 gallon Mexican style beans
1 gallon diced tomatoes
2 8-oz. cans tomato sauce
4 4-oz. cans tomato paste
1 gallon water
salt
pepper
chili powder
minced garlic

Brown hamburger, green pepper, onion and celery. Drain and add beans. Add tomatoes, tomato sauce and paste, and water. Add salt, pepper, chili powder and minced garlic to make a mild flavor. Bring to boil and then simmer.

ROAST PORK

Al Buda, Former Chef, Blackstone Hotel
Omaha, NE

Make marinade of:
1 cup soy sauce
1 cup pineapple juice
2 tbsp. brown sugar
1 tsp. ground cinnamon
1 oz. bourbon

Pour over pork tenderloin and marinate in refrigerator 12 to 15 hours. Roast as long as weight of meat requires.

PARTY PICKLES

Maxine Bossellman, Bossellman's
Grand Island, NE

1 quart home-style dills (no garlic)
2¾ cups sugar
½ cup dark vinegar
2 heaping tbsp. pickling spices (in net bag)

Drain pickles, cut into chunks and put in large bowl. Add sugar, vinegar and spices. Stir often and next day put back in jar. Throw away spice bag.

TRAIL DRIVE SWISS STEAK

Norine Stewart, Chief Restaurant
McCook, NE

Serves 25:
5 lbs. inside round
1 tbsp. salt
4 cups flour
1 lb. shortening
½ tbsp. pepper

Cut steak into 5 oz. pieces and tenderize very well. Mix flour, salt and pepper together and dredge steak through mixture. Brown steaks.

4 lbs. green pepper
3 lbs. onion
4 lbs. celery
Cut in large chunks.
#10 can diced tomatoes
2 48-oz. cans tomato juice
1 cup flour

Combine green pepper, celery, onion and diced tomatoes. Mix tomato juice and flour together; combine with vegetables. Heat sauce and vegetables to boiling point. Layer in pan, alternating between sauce and steaks, with sauce as the top and bottom layer. Bake at 325° for 2 hours.

JANIE STEEL'S PIE CRUST

Norine Stewart, Chief Restaurant
McCook, NE

1¼ cup lard (or shortening)
3 cups flour
1 tsp. salt
2 tbsp. sugar
1 egg
⅓ cup water
2 tbsp. lemon juice or vinegar

Cut lard into flour, salt and sugar. Beat egg and add to water with lemon juice or vinegar. Stir into flour mixture and chill before rolling out crusts.

SUNRISE FRITATA

James Parthemore III, Cornhusker Hotel
Lincoln, NE

grated Romano cheese—1 tsp. for each fritata
3 eggs for each fritata mixed with
1 oz. heavy whipping cream

Finely chop and blanch the following vegetables for each fritata:

1 floret broccoli
1 floret cauliflower
2 slices carrot
2 slices yellow squash
2 slices green pepper
2 slices red pepper

Finely chop 2 black olives for each fritata for garnish on top.

2 thin slices mozzarella cheese
approximately 3 oz. tomato sauce
3 pinches finely chopped fresh basil
salt to taste
ground black pepper to taste
1 pinch oregano
1 tbsp. butter

Mix eggs, cream, grated cheese and spices. Whip together. Heat butter in a non-stick omelette pan. Cook egg mixture as you would to prepare an omelette. Prepare a flat omelette and place on warm plate. Next place blanched vegetables onto the eggs and spread out like for a pizza. Encircle edges with tomato sauce, top with mozzarella cheese, melt under broiler and sprinkle chopped olives on top.

CAJUN BEER
BATTERED PHEASANT

Randy Stewart, McCook Elks Club
McCook, NE

6 pheasant breasts, boned and skinned
2 bottles Heineken beer
4 tbsp. cajun quick spicy chicken seasoning (Schillings)
4 cups all purpose flour

Mix flour and beer together so that you have a thick pancake consistency. Add cajun spice. Coat pheasant breast and pan fry until golden brown. Place on tray on top shelf of oven for ½ hour at 200° until tender. Serves 3 persons.

SPICY ORIENTAL
PORK RIBLETS

5 lbs. pork ribs — not "country style"
2 lg. bottles teriyaki marinade and sauce (La Choy)
2 tsp. ground ginger
2 tsp. garlic
1 bottle cajun quick seasoning
1 diced onion
3 bottles hoisin sauce

Place whole ribs in glass baking dish. Don't cut up ribs! Add all ingredients except cajun spice and soak overnight covered in the refrigerator. Start charcoal fire and brown ribs till about half done on each side. (Season ribs with cajun seasoning before you grill them.) Cut ribs and layer them in glass baking dish. Pour hoisin sauce over them and bake for about 1 hour at 300° covered. Should feed six people if you keep out of them!

SHRIMP ON THE GRILL

Timothy M. Frank, The French Cafe
Omaha, NE

Marinade:
2 cups white wine
4 tbsp. Worcestershire
3 cloves garlic, roughly chopped
1 tbsp. dried rosemary or 2 branches fresh

Combine all ingredients in stainless steel or plastic bowl.
2 lbs. shrimp (shell on)

Split shrimp from the front to the back leaving shell on. Rinse out vein. Cover with marinade and marinate 3 hours to overnight.

Cook shrimp over medium coals until pink and opaque. Approximately 5 minutes.

GARLIC AND HERB SAUCE

1 roasted red pepper, finely chopped
1 roasted green bell pepper, finely chopped
1 tbsp. rosemary
1 clove of garlic
juice of ½ lemon
1½ cups Hellman's mayonnaise

Put all ingredients in food processor or blender and process. Use as a dip for shrimp.

MARVEL'S FRESH LEMON BARS

Ron Popp, The Garden Cafe
Omaha, NE

3 cups flour
1 cup powdered sugar
1½ cups soft butter

Mix and pat out as a crust in 9 x 13 pan.

8 eggs
4 cups sugar
1 cup lemon juice
½ cup flour
1 tsp. baking powder
2 tsp. vanilla
½ tsp. salt

Mix and pour over crust. Bake till firm in center. Low oven, 340-350° about 45 minutes to 1 hour. Top with powdered sugar, chill and serve.

GREGG'S SOUR CREAM APPLE PIE

Peel 7 Granny Smith apples, cut into slices, sprinkle with lemon juice. To the apples, add:

1¼ cups sugar
⅔ cup flour
½ tsp. salt
1 tsp. cinnamon
¼ tsp. nutmeg
⅓ cup soft butter

Mix thoroughly with the apples. Pour into an unbaked pie shell. It will be stacked high. Atop the apple mixture, spread a heaping cup of sour cream. Bake at 350° for 90-110 minutes.

ENGLISH TRIFLE

Bruce Sampson, Jax Shack
Lincoln, NE

1. Make a pound cake. Cream 2 cups butter; add 2 cups sugar and cream again. Beat in 9 eggs, one at a time. Add 2 tsp. vanilla; sift and measure 4 cups flour and add slowly to above. Pour into a 10″ tube pan, greased and floured. Bake 1 hour at 325°. After pound cake has cooled, cut into 1″ squares and place in bottom of 11 x 13 pan, one layer thick. Use as much of the cake as possible.

2. Sprinkle ½ cup brandy over cake.

3. Cover cake and brandy with any good strawberry or raspberry preserves; about ¼″ thick. Then slice fresh strawberries and cover preserves with these.

4. Mix up 2 boxes of vanilla pudding and pour over the top; chill until set.

5. To serve, dish up with ice cream scoop and place in margarita glass with pudding on top. You may top with whipped cream or cognac sauce.

6. To make cognac sauce, cream together 8 tbsp. butter and two cups powdered sugar; gradually add ¼ cup cognac. Whip until the consistency of whipped cream.

AMARETTO TRUFFLES

C. Floridia, LaStrada 72
Omaha, NE

12 1 oz. squares semi-sweet chocolate
½ cup butter or margarine
2 egg yolks
½ cup whipping cream
¼ cup amaretto liqueur
finely chopped almonds

Place chocolate in top of double boiler; bring water to a boil. Reduce heat to low; cook until chocolate melts. Remove from heat; add butter 1 tbsp. at a time.

Beat egg yolks at medium speed until thick and lemon-colored. Gradually stir in ¼ of hot mixture; stirring constantly.

Stir in whipping cream and amaretto. Add mixture to chocolate.

Return to heat and cook 1 minute or until thick and smooth, stirring constantly.

Cover and chill at least 8 hours or until firm. Shape mixture into 1″ balls; roll in chopped almonds or chocolate sprinkles. Store in refrigerator. Makes about 3 dozen.

TORTA DI RHUM & CHOCOLATTE

C. Floridia, LaStrada 72
Omaha, NE

2 1 oz. squares unsweeted chocolate
½ cup water
½ cup butter, softened
1¾ cups sifted cake flour
1½ cups firmly packed light brown sugar
3 eggs
1½ tsp. baking powder
½ tsp. baking soda
¼ tsp. salt
¼ cup rum

Grease cake pans to be used; line with wax paper and grease again. Set aside.

Combine chocolate and water in small saucepan; place over low heat, stirring until chocolate melts. Set aside to cool.

Cream butter, gradually add sugar, beating well at medium speed. Add eggs, one at a time, beating well after each addition.

Combine flour, baking powder, soda and salt. Add to creamed mixture alternately with chocolate. Mix well after each addition. Stir in rum.

Spoon batter into prepared pans. Bake at 350° for 20-25 minutes.

Cool 5 minutes; remove from pan, cool on wire racks without liners.

(See next page for Frosting.)

CHOCOLATE RUM FROSTING

C. Floridia, LaStrada 72
Omaha, NE

3 tbsp. semisweet chocolate morsels
1½ (1 oz.) squares unsweetened chocolate
1 tbsp. butter or margarine
1 cup powdered sugar
1 egg
2 tbsp. milk
2 tbsp. rum

Combine chocolate and butter in top of double boiler; bring water to a boil. Reduce heat to low; cook until chocolate melts.

Combine powdered sugar, egg, milk and rum; mix until smooth. Stir in chocolate mixture. Place bowl in larger bowl of ice water; beat until thick and fluffy.

Enough to cover 2 9″ layers.

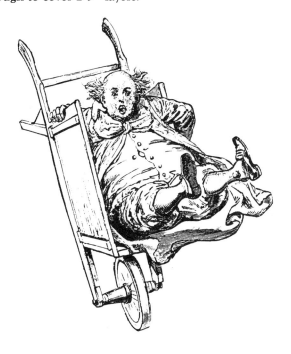

HONEY LEMON
YOGURT DRESSING

Martin Prettyman, LePeep
Omaha NE

2 cups plain yogurt
6 tbsp. honey
½ tsp. fresh grated lemon peel

Wash a lemon well; using a hand grater, grate the lemon peel onto a plate. Measure amount needed and add to the plain yogurt. Add honey and stir.

Best if made 24 hours in advance. Excellent used as a dip for fresh fruit sections.

LEMONY DILL
DRESSING

4 cups mayonnaise
1½ cup half and half
¼ cup Parmesan cheese
¼ cup fresh lemon juice
½ tsp. garlic powder
½ tsp. white pepper
½ tsp. black pepper
1/8 tsp. cayenne pepper
1/8 tsp. dill weed

Combine all ingredients and blend with a wire whip. This dressing holds very well in refrigerator. Thin with half and half when needed at a later date. It becomes very thick.

SPLIT PEA SOUP

Moby's
Bloomfield, NE

8 cups washed peas
1½ gallons water
4 tbsp. ham base
3 tbsp. Moby's Surf & Turf seasoning
1 tbsp. Kitchen Bouquet
2 cups diced onion
2 cups diced celery
3 grated carrots
1 lb. diced ham
½ tsp. thyme

Simmer until peas are tender. Stir frequently. Serve with croutons. Makes 2 gallons.

RATATOUILLE

Kay Brestel, K's Restaurant
Lincoln, NE

2 tbsp. oil
1 eggplant
1 green pepper, diced
¼ cup chopped parsley
½ tsp. rosemary and thyme
1 lb. sliced onion
1 lb. sliced tomato
1 lb. sliced zucchini
1 lb. sliced mushrooms
2 cloves garlic, minced
1 tbsp. sage
1 tsp. salt

Put oil in saucepan and add vegetables in layers, sprinkling herbs, garlic and salt throughout. Simmer over low heat covered for 2 hours until cooked. Serve hot over a bed of rice with grated cheese. Cook for less time if you like more firm vegetables.

BREAKFAST IN A PAN

O'Doherty's Dining and Saloon
Crawford, NE

Grease a 2 inch deep large baking dish or pan. Cube French bread sliced thin. Cover bottom of pan with cubes and butter. Add layer of ham chunks and grated cheddar cheese. Layer twice. Beat 16 eggs, 1½-2 cups milk, salt and pepper. Pour over top. Add extra milk if needed. Sprinkle lightly with paprika. Cover with foil and refrigerate overnight. Bake at 350° for 1½ hours. Uncover last ½ hour. Serves 8-10. A marvelous souffle texture and an incredible flavor.

Ed. Note: I made this Christmas Eve for Christmas morning and it was everything it was cracked up (16 eggs) to be! However, I should mention that 6 of us demolished the whole thing.

PEPPERCORN FETTUCCINE WITH OYSTERS AND PINK CHAMPAGNE SAUCE

Paul Jorgenson and Joe Miller, P.J.'s
Lincoln, NE

2 servings—

Pasta:
¾ cup all purpose flour
2 tbsp. semolina flour
1 tsp. dried pink peppercorns, crushed

salt
freshly ground pepper
1 egg
1 tbsp. water
1 tbsp. vegetable oil

Prepare as you would any pasta — or you may use your own frozen pasta.

Champagne Sauce:
1 cup brut rose or blanc de noir champagne
¼ tsp. crushed tarragon
½ tsp. sugar
2 small zucchini
1 large zucchini
3 tbsp. butter
salt and pepper
8 fresh oysters (liquor reserved)

For pasta: cook until al dente; sprinkle with crushed peppercorns and tarragon. Combine with melted butter. Set aside and keep warm.

For sauce: boil first three ingredients in heavy saucepan until liquid is reduced by half. Reduce to low heat. Add oysters and cook until just opaque. Transfer oysters to bowl. Drain any liquid from oysters into poaching liquid. Add reserved oyster liquid; boil until reduced to 2 tbsp.

Cut skin from two small zucchini in long strips. Using oval melon baller, scoop out 8 ovals. Melt 2 tbsp. butter in pan. Add ovals and cook until lightly browned. Transfer ovals to warm plate. Saute strips of zucchini, add to platter.

Bring reduced poaching liquid to simmer. Remove from heat and wisk in 2 tbsp. butter. Add oysters. Arrange pasta on serving plate, add ovals and oysters; pour sauce over all. Garnish with zucchini strips.

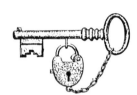

WHO'S WHO?

In the process of collecting menu material for this cookbook, several recipes were received from people I don't know. I'm grateful for the interest and glad to include them. I also look forward to meeting the authors of same sometime soon.

P.S. To Whom It May Concern: Please identify yourself and your recipe, or Orr will be lost!.

ZIPPY BLADE STEAK

William B. Cassel
Ainsworth, NE

round steak cut ¾" thick
3 tbsp. soy sauce
3 tbsp. vinegar
2 tbsp. salad oil
2 tbsp. catsup
1/8 tsp. garlic powder

Combine soy sauce, vinegar, oil, catsup and garlic powder
in a plastic bag. Place steak in bag and coat both sides with
liquid. Close bag tightly and marinate steak in refrigerator
at least 6 hours or overnight. Turn at least once. Grill or broil
to desired doneness (rare to medium). Cut crossgrain into
thin slices.

SWEET AND SOUR MUSTARD

Patrick Duncan
Franklin, NE

1 cup apple cider vinegar
2 oz. can of Coleman's dry mustard

Mix the above in a glass jar, cover and let stand at least 12 hours; 24 is OK.

Put in saucepan with:

1 cup sugar
2 well-beaten eggs

Cook until it thickens, stirring while cooking. (Can be microwaved.)

Makes about a pint. Will get thicker in the refrigerator.

WDO: Being a mustard aficionado, I can hardly wait to try this. Can you imagine how good it would be on bratwurst or Polish?

LEMON BREAD

These little loaves make great gifts...

Mabel Durand
Loretto, NE

1½ cups sugar
1⅔ cups flour
2 tsp. baking powder
¼ tsp. salt

Sift above ingredients together.

Beat 6 whole eggs, add 1 cup salad oil and the rind of two lemons grated fine. Add dry ingredients. Bake at 350⁰ for 30 minutes.

Makes 3 small loaves.

BOHEMIAN BRISKET

Tom Lauvetz, Owner/Manager, Imperial Mall
Hastings, NE

2 lbs. trimmed brisket
6 medium onions, sliced
¼ tsp. salt
dash pepper
dash thyme
1 bay leaf
1 cup boiling water
½ lb. honey
1 stale piece rye bread
juice of 1 lemon

Place meat in heavy kettle (I use large frying pan); add onions, salt, pepper, thyme, and bay leaf. Add boiling water and simmer until meat is almost done, add honey and stir frequently while cooking. Be careful not to let it burn.

Soak bread in a little water, mash, and, when thoroughly softened, add to meat. Stir well; add 2 additional cups water and the lemon juice.

Cook until meat is very well browned. Serves 6.

Note: I cook the brisket for several hours before I add the honey and bread. Excellent served with dumplings and sauerkraut.

FIRST CLASS MICHELOB BBQ SAUCE

Terrific on ribs, chicken and barbequed ground beef...keeps for weeks and actually improves with age.

Les Lawless, Owner, Lawless Distributing
Hastings, NE

2 tbsp. bacon drippings
1 medium onion, chopped fine
1 clove garlic, minced
½ cup celery, chopped fine
3 tbsp. brown sugar
1½ cups catsup
¼ cup cider vinegar
¼ cup Michelob beer*
¼ cup Worcestershire sauce
¼ tsp. salt
1 tsp. mustard
dash pepper
½ cup water
Tabasco sauce to taste
½ tsp. liquid smoke

Melt bacon drippings in saucepan and saute the onion, celery and garlic until transparent. Add all remaining ingredients except liquid smoke. Bring to a boil, add liquid smoke and simmer gently for 15 minutes. Remove from heat and cool. Pour into a jar and refrigerate. Makes about 3 cups.

*WDO: *Why not drink the rest of the bottle while cooking sauce?*

GRILLED STEAK WITH ONIONS AND MUSHROOMS

We like our steak cooked medium and think this meat is super good.

Milford Nelson
Grand Island, NE

4 lb. sirloin steak about 2″ thick
⅔ cup olive oil
⅓ cup red wine vinegar
salt and pepper to taste
1 clove garlic, minced
½ tsp. oregano
4 tbsp. butter
2 large onions, sliced into rings
1 lb. fresh mushrooms, sliced
1 onion, chopped

Trim steak of excess fat; score the edge at 1″ intervals. Place in shallow glass dish.

In a small bowl, mix oil, vinegar, salt, pepper, garlic, chopped onion and oregano. Pour over steak; cover with plastic wrap and marinate a couple of hours.

Over a medium fire, grill steak 5-6″ from heat, brushing several times with marinade. Cook 15 minutes on each side for rare, 20 minutes for medium and about 25 minutes for well-done.

While steak is cooking, melt butter in large skillet and saute onion rings and mushrooms.

When steak has cooked, allow to sit for 10 minutes, then slice. Serve with sauteed onions and mushrooms. Serves 8.

CHEESECAKE

A "crusty" variety for those of you who prefer it that way.
Dave Parker, Attorney
Lincoln, NE

---

12 oz. cream cheese, softened
2 beaten eggs
½ cup sugar
1 tsp. vanilla

Beat together.
Line pan with a graham cracker crust made of:

---

20 crushed crackers
3 tbsp. melted butter

Pour in filling and bake at 325° for 30 minutes. Cool.
Spread with mixture of:

½ pt. sour cream
2 tbsp. sugar

Bake an additional 5-10 minutes at 325°.
Serve cold. Serves 8.

WDO: We received LOTS of recipes for cheesecake and selected several that were each a little different than the others. You may want to try them all! To help you find them faster, you can look in the alphabetical index by food type at the end of the book. Or, if you're not in a hurry, just browse through the whole book and make note of the page numbers as you go!

HE-MAN QUICHE

Real men do TOO...and I've never met one who didn't like this version.

Nick Rambour, Owner, Rambour Realty Company
Columbus, NE

Crust:
2½ cups seasoned croutons, crushed
¼ cup margarine, melted

Filling:
6 tbsp. Parmesan cheese, grated
10 oz. package frozen chopped spinach,
thawed and drained
1 cup small curd cottage cheese
4 oz. monterey jack cheese, cut into small pieces
3 eggs, beaten
2 tbsp. sour cream
¼ cup chopped onion
1 clove garlic, minced
1 cup ham, cubed
½ tsp. salt (optional)

Preheat oven to 350°. Combine crushed croutons with melted margarine (or butter). Mix well and press into bottom and sides of a 9 or 10″ pie plate. Set aside.

To make filling, combine 2 tsp. of Parmesan cheese with spinach, cottage cheese, monterey jack cheese, eggs, onions, sour cream, garlic, ham and salt. Mix until well-blended. Spoon mixture into prepared crust. Bake uncovered at 350° for 40 minutes or until set. Sprinkle with remaining Parmesan cheese. Let stand 5 minutes before serving.

WDO: I've never had any arguments about manhood or quiche or any combination thereof. I'm with Nick—think this sounds great.

CHOCOLATE CHIP COOKIES

Probably the world's favorite kind of cookie...overall.
LeRoy Trofholz, President, Wagner Mills
Schuyler, NE

½ cup shortening
1 tsp. vanilla
½ cup sugar
½ cup brown sugar
1 well-beaten egg
1½ cups flour
½ tsp. salt
½ tsp. baking soda
7 oz. package semi-sweet chocolate chips
½ cup chopped walnuts

Cream shortening, vanilla and sugars. Add egg. Beat well. Add dry ingredients. Stir in chocolate chips and nuts. Chill. Drop on greased cookie sheets. Bake 10 to 12 minutes at 375°.

WDO: I refuse to get into a cookie controversy about what is the best, most popular, etc. I'm already embroiled in one situation with peanut butter sandwiches...and that's sticky enough.

Gene Spence (back row center) and his fellow Old Vienna Chowder Club gang—looks fun(ky) to me.

Del Weber— looks like he has more sugar on his face than in the bowl; I always thought he was a sweet guy.

Dallen Peterson-Super Chef...his apron even says so.

PRODUCTION CREW

This book could not have been assembled by yours truly alone. These people helped to make it possible, along with a lot of other "pros" from their companies. Without them, there would be no cookbook beyond the one in my head.

SCALLOPED CORN

Originally prepared when I was in 4-H, this has become a family favorite, and it appears on the table at most get-togethers.
Ann Andrejack, Secretary to Bill Orr
Woodmen Accident and Life, Lincoln, NE

1 #303 can cream style corn
½ cup cracker crumbs (10-12 soda crackers)
¼ cup chopped onion (2 tbsp. if dried)
¼ cup chopped green pepper (2 tbsp. if dried)
½ cup milk
1 egg, slightly beaten
¼ tsp. salt
1/8 tsp. pepper
1 tbsp. margarine

Preheat oven to 350°. Mix above ingredients together except margarine and place in greased baking dish. Dot with margarine. Bake uncovered for 30 minutes. Serves 4.

WDO: Ann has donated countless hours to this cookbook. She is my personal secretary, a good friend and a good cook!

WILD RICE SOUP

This really IS my favorite!

David T. Calhoun, President,
Jacob North Printing Company
Lincoln, NE

¾ cup uncooked wild rice
1 can beef boullion
2 cups water

Cook rice in above liquids about 45 minutes or until tender. While rice is cooking, combine in large soup pot:

2 cans mushroom soup
2 cans chicken broth
2 cups fresh sauteed mushrooms
3 cups half and half

Fry ½ lb. diced bacon to medium crisp. Saute ½ cup diced celery and 2 diced carrots in bacon fat. Drain any excess fat. Add to above mixture along with rice when done. Heat thoroughly, but do NOT let it boil!

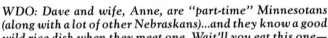

WDO: Dave and wife, Anne, are "part-time" Minnesotans (along with a lot of other Nebraskans)...and they know a good wild rice dish when they meet one. Wait'll you eat this one—it's perfect for a soup supper on a cold winter night.

TWICE BAKED POTATOES

Brennan's Restaurant in New Orleans gets credit for the basic ingredients...I've changed the measurements some over the years.

Pam Eiche, Vice President (retired),
Ayres and Associates
Lincoln, NE

Bake potatoes in oven or microwave until mealy. While still hot, scoop out the center white portions, leaving enough potato on "shell" so it won't collapse.

For EACH potato you are baking:

Fry one strip of bacon till crisp
Saute one chopped green onion till it starts to get limp

Crumble bacon and drain with onion on paper towels.

In separate bowl, for EACH potato, combine:

1 tbsp. grated Parmesan cheese
2 tbsp. sour cream
dash of white pepper

Mix drained bacon/onion, cheese/cream with potato stuffing till it reaches the consistency of your choice. (Some people like to whip it until very smooth, others like to leave it sorta chunky.) If you do want it more "whipped", you may have to add more sour cream. An electric mixer is practically a must for this...unless you're heavy into building up your arm muscles.

Restuff potato shells, pour melted butter or margarine over tops and dust with paprika.* Bake at 350° about 20 minutes or until hot.

* Can be done up to this stage and refrigerated or frozen for later use. If cold, they will have to bake slightly longer.

WDO: Pam was very fortunate to "find" Fred Eiche. Fred was even more fortunate to find Pam. Had I not discovered the two of them, this cookbook would not be in print today. Pam was our advertising agency Account Executive for many years. During that time she and I worked together on several projects. That was fun, but not nearly as much fun as this cookbook. I will be eternally grateful.

COCKTAIL POTATOES

Thank goodness—a different hors d'ouevre than the usual fare...
Julie Seever, Account Executive
Jacob North Printing Co.

---

2 lbs. small new red potatoes (1½″ diameter)
sour cream

Boil potatoes in lightly salted water. Do not overcook. Drain and cool to room temperature. Cut potatoes in half and using a melon baller, scoop out the mounded top and place on a serving platter.

Put a dollop of sour cream on each potato ball and garnish with various items such as caviar, chives, fresh ground pepper, etc.

❧

WDO: Rumor has it that this woman is a first-rate cook, though I've not had the first-hand experience to confirm it. She certainly is a first-class print expert and was of monumental help in getting this book published.

BERNEAL'S
SCRAMBLE SNACK

Long before the popular cereal snack mixes became famous, my mother made this every Christmas. We have continued to do so. It makes a LOT. Even so, with two grown sons at home for the holidays last year, Ruthie and I made it twice so their sister and we could get a taste.

Dick Young, Chairman of the Board
Ayres and Associates Inc.
Lincoln, NE

---

2 lbs. salted mixed nuts (mostly Deluxe)
12 oz. wheat Chex
10½ oz. Cheerios
16½ oz. rice Chex
10 oz. slim pretzel stix
2 cups vegetable oil
2 tbsp. Worcestershire sauce
1 tbsp. garlic salt
1 tbsp. seasoning salt

Mix all ingredients in an extra-large roaster or a 13 qt. metal bowl. Bake at 250° for 2 hours, stirring carefully with a wooden spoon every 15 minutes.

❧

WDO: Dick enjoys stirring things up now and then. This is his favorite because he gets to taste it at each stirring. After two hours' samplings, no wonder they had to make 2 batches (26 qts.)!

Chancellor and Mrs. Martin Massengale
amidst the main course.

Joan and Bob Kayton—must be Thousand
Smile-nd Dressing.

Charley and Ruthie Thone, western-style.

Vickie and Roman Hruska palavering
in the kitchen.

A MEAL
IN ITSELF

Two Omaha couples, the Werners
and the Wickershams, really got into
the spirit of this thing and created
recipes for a whole meal. We were so
impressed by their enthusiasm, not to
mention the delectable-sounding
menu, we decided to include the
whole thing "as is". Kay and I are anx-
iously awaiting an invitation to such
a dinner...and hope it will be in one
of the Werner's homes...preferably the
"little grass shack" in Hawaii.

Clarence Werner and Gale Wickersham – what a pair to dine with.

POTATO SOUP

Gale Wickersham

6-8 red potatoes
salt and pepper
1 large bermuda onion
4 pork chops, fat removed
1 can evaporated milk
3 tbsp. butter

Boil 8 cups of water, lightly salted. Add potatoes and the onion, diced. Add 4 diced pork chops plus bones. Cook over medium heat until potatoes are very soft, about 45 minutes. Remove bones. If desired, mash some of the potatoes for thicker consistency. Add the evaporated milk (PET) and 3 tbsp. butter. Stir well and continue cooking for 5 minutes. Season to taste. Serve with crackers, grated cheese or bacon bits as garnish.

HOT SPINACH SALAD

Gale Wickersham

2 lg. bunches spinach
6 slices thick bacon
6 stalks green onion
⅓ cup red wine vinegar
¼ cup burgundy wine
4 tbsp. granulated sugar
pepper

In large skillet, brown minced bacon. Drain off all grease and add minced green onion. Continue cooking on low heat a couple of minutes. Add to skillet red wine vinegar and the burgundy wine. Stir in sugar and cook over very low heat 5 minutes. Have ready, cleaned, drained and torn fresh spinach leaves. Just before serving, pour hot dressing over spinach and toss well. Serve and garnish with chopped cooked egg, fresh mushroom slices, croutons, thin sliced red onion or tomato.

WHITE WINE
SCALLOPS

You may notice that this recipe contains no salt! That's right.
Gale Wickersham, President
Dorsey Trailer Sales
Omaha, NE

3 lbs. fresh or frozen scallops
1 tbsp. butter
1 fresh whole lemon
1 cup white wine
pepper

Rinse off sea scallops and leave to drain on paper towels.

On griddle cooking surface, wok or large metal skillet, melt butter. Add the scallops and top slowly with half of the lemon squeezed and half the white wine. Cook over low heat 10-12 minutes. Finish adding the remaining white wine and drizzle with lemon juice. Scallops are done when white throughout. Serve immediately.

VEGETABLE GRILL

Goes great with the scallops...

Clarence Werner, Chairman
Werner Enterprises
Omaha, NE

1 red pepper
1 green pepper
1 yellow pepper
4 small red potatoes
1 zucchini
1 white onion
1 cup pineapple chunks

Cut everything but potatoes in 1″ chunks. Slice potato wedges ½″ thick. Marinate in ¾ cup olive oil (extra light), 1 tsp. sesame oil, 3 chopped cloves of garlic and lemon pepper. Split in half and put in 12″ vegetable grill basket. Grill 8-10 minutes on each side. For variety, you can splash vegetables with teriyaki sauce.

STUFFED SALMON

Clarence Werner

---

4 lb. salmon, deboned and open on one side
1 package mushroom/wild rice
Stove Top Select Stuffing
½ lemon
dash pepper

Squeeze lemon juice over cavity, sprinkle with pepper and stuff.

Grill in fish basket for 12 minutes on each side.

PEACH-AMARETTO ICE CREAM

This is a favorite at the annual Arizona Dove Hunt when peaches are their freshest.

Clarence Werner

4 eggs
1 cup sugar
2 tbsp. vanilla
½ pt. whipping cream
2 cans Eagle Brand condensed milk
dairy milk
¼ tsp. salt

Combine eggs, sugar, salt and vanilla in bowl and mix thoroughly with mixer. Pour into freezer can, add condensed milk and stir well. Add 1 cup peeled fresh peaches chopped fine and dairy milk to fill line on can. Stir. Process according to directions on freezer. Garnish with a splash of amaretto and serve with Pepperidge Farm Pirouettes.

DINNER
AT THE
WHITE HOUSE

During Kay's term as Governor, we have been privileged to share several meals with President Reagan. During one National Governors' Association meeting, I sat next to Mrs. Reagan at lunch. At a later dinner, I sat next to then Vice President Bush. Kay was seated next to President Reagan on more than one occasion, including his final State Dinner in honor of Margaret Thatcher. To say these occasions were memorable experiences is somewhat of an understatement. I thought you might like to share a little look at the scrapbook from The State Dinner, so what follows is a reprint of the menu, along with a photo and (you know me!) a story...or two.

DINNER

Honoring The Right Honorable
The Prime Minister of the United Kingdom
of Great Britain and Northern Ireland
and Mr. Thatcher

Baby Lobster Bellevue
Caviar Yogurt Sauce
Curried Croissant

Roasted Saddle of Veal Périgourdine
Jardinière of Vegetables
Asparagus with Hazelnut Butter

Autumn Mixed Salad
Selection of Cheese

Chestnut Marquise
Pistachio Sauce
Orange Tuiles and Ginger Twigs

SAINTSBURY *Chardonnay 1987*
STAG'S LEAP WINE CELLARS *Cabernet Sauvignon 1978*
SCHRAMSBERG *Crémant Demi-Sec 1984*

THE WHITE HOUSE
Wednesday, November 16, 1988

President Reagan visited Nebraska three times during Kay's campaign and first two years in office. The first two visits were a direct result of her invitations. (I'm not too sure anyone else could have talked him into stopping at North Platte on his way to California.) Ronald Reagan and I, therefore, have at least two things in common: 1) neither of us can refuse Kay and 2) ...I can't remember the second one...

Riding in the Presidential Limousine with President Reagan and his Chief of Staff, Kay and I were delighted to listen to the President's anecdotes. Upon arrival in Omaha on Air Force One, stepping out of the plane and into the Limousine, President Reagan said, "Being here in Nebraska reminds me of a story. Come to think of it, at my age, everything reminds me of a story!"

And then there's the "keeping it all in perspective" story...

Following Kay's election and prior to her inauguration, we went on a well-deserved week's vacation. Upon returning home (we had not yet moved into the Governor's Mansion), we found the following note from our cleaning lady.

> "Kay: Andy Card, Special Assistant to the President, called to invite The Governor to breakfast next Tuesday morning. If you can be there Monday night, the Vice President will invite you to dinner. The event at The White House will be finished by 2:00 Tuesday. Please call him back. I am out of Comet and stool cleanser. Thanks—"

First Gentleman puts finishing touches on favorite dish.

INDEX BY RECIPE

BREAKFAST/BRUNCH

CASSEROLES/ONE DISH MEALS

CAKES, PASTRY, PIES

POULTRY

SALADS

SALAD DRESSINGS

SANDWICHES

SAUCES, JAM, JELLY

SAUCES, JAM, JELLY

SOUPS

VEAL, LAMB

VEGETABLES & SIDE DISHES

INDEX BY CONTRIBUTOR

RESTAURANT INDEX

For the not-so-enthusiastic dieter, this list of calorie-burning activities from the Southern California Medical Association may be just what you're looking for. These will give you a whole new slant on calorie counting.

Beating around the bush 75
Jumping to conclusions 100
Swallowing your pride...........................50
Climbing the walls 150
Throwing your weight around........50-300*
Dragging your heels............................100
Pushing your luck 250
Making mountains out of molehills 500
Adding fuel to the fire 150
Hitting the nail on the head.................50

* depending on your weight

— The End —

Please print or type and mail order with payment to:
    First Gentleman's Cookbook,
    Governor's Mansion,
    Lincoln, NE 68508

Please send _____ copies of Bill Orr's Cookbook
    @ $12.50 each (Tax deductible) _____

Plus postage and handling @ $2.50 each _____

Nebraska residents please add sales tax of $ .76 for each book _____

Enclosed is my check or money order for **TOTAL** _____

NAME_____

ADDRESS_____

CITY_____ STATE_____ ZIP_____

Please print or type and mail order with payment to:
    First Gentleman's Cookbook,
    Governor's Mansion,
    Lincoln, NE 68508

Please send _____ copies of Bill Orr's Cookbook
    @ $12.50 each (Tax deductible) _____

Plus postage and handling @ $2.50 each _____

Nebraska residents please add sales tax of $ .76 for each book _____

Enclosed is my check or money order for **TOTAL** _____

NAME_____

ADDRESS_____

CITY_____ STATE_____ ZIP_____

Please print or type and mail order with payment to:
    First Gentleman's Cookbook,
    Governor's Mansion,
    Lincoln, NE 68508

Please send _____ copies of Bill Orr's Cookbook
    @ $12.50 each (Tax deductible) _____

Plus postage and handling @ $2.50 each _____

Nebraska residents please add sales tax of $ .76 for each book _____

Enclosed is my check or money order for **TOTAL** _____

NAME_____

ADDRESS_____

CITY_____ STATE_____ ZIP_____